ALL THUMBS
Guide to
Home Plumbing

Other All Thumbs Guides
Home Wiring
Painting, Wallpapering and Stenciling
Repairing Major Home Appliances

All Thumbs

Guide to
Home Plumbing

Robert W. Wood
Illustrations by Steve Hoeft

TAB BOOKS

Blue Ridge Summit, PA

FIRST EDITION
SECOND PRINTING

© 1992 by **TAB Books**.
TAB Books is a division of McGraw-Hill, Inc.

Library of Congress Cataloging-in-Publication Data

Wood, Robert W., 1933-
    All thumbs guide to home plumbing / by Robert W. Wood.
        p.   cm.
    Includes index.
    ISBN 0-8306-2546-1   ISBN 0-8306-2545-3 (pbk.)
    1. Plumbing—Amateurs' manuals.   I. Title
    TH6124.W66 1992   91-41376
    696'.1—dc20   CIP

Acquisitions Editor: Kimberly Tabor
Designer: Jaclyn J. Boone
Editorial Team: Carol H. Munson, Editor
                Susan D. Wahlman
                Joanne Slike

Production Team: Katherine G. Brown, Director of Production
                  Janice Ridenour, Layout
                  Jana L. Fisher, Typesetting
Cover Design: Lori E. Schlosser
Cover Illustration: Denny Bond, East Petersburg, PA
Cartoon Caricatures: Michael Malle, Pittsburgh, PA   ATS

The All Thumbs Guarantee

TAB Books/McGraw-Hill guarantees that you will be able to follow every step of each project in this book, from beginning to end, or you will receive your money back. If you are unable to follow the All Thumbs steps, return this book, your store receipt, and a brief explanation to:

All Thumbs
P.O. Box 581
Blue Ridge Summit, PA 17214-9998

About the Binding

This and every All Thumbs book has a special lay-flat binding. To take full advantage of this binding, open the book to any page and run your finger along the spine, pressing down as you do so; the book will stay open at the page you've selected.

The lay-flat binding is designed to withstand constant use. Unlike regular book bindings, the spine will not weaken or crack when you press down on the spine to keep the book open.

Contents

Preface

A collection of books about do-it-yourself home repair and improvement, the All Thumbs series was created not for the skilled jack-of-all-trades, but for the average homeowner. If your familiarity with the various systems in the home is minimal, or your budget doesn't keep pace with today's climbing costs, this series is tailor-made for you.

Several different types of professional contractors are required to construct even the smallest home. Carpenters build the framework, plumbers install the pipes, and electricians complete the wiring. Few people can do it all. The necessary skills often require years to master. The professional works quickly and efficiently and depends on a large volume of work to survive. Because service calls are time-consuming, often requiring more travel time than actual labor, they can be expensive. The All Thumbs series saves you time and money by showing you how to make most common repairs yourself.

The guides cover topics such as home wiring; plumbing; painting, stenciling, and wallpapering; and repairing major appliances, to name a few. Copiously illustrated, each book details the procedures in an easy-to-follow, step-by-step format, making many repairs and home improvements well within the ability of nearly any homeowner.

Introduction

Designed for the novice do-it-yourselfer, this book will provide relief from the frustrating problems that crop up in the home plumbing system. It was written because of the mind-jarring drip of a faucet that keeps you awake at night, the annoying sound of a toilet that's still running as you settle back in front of the TV, and the garbage disposal that only hums when you flip the switch.

Starting with the basics here in the Introduction, this book shows the skeletal framework of a typical home and exposes the internal plumbing system. Chapter 1 presents a systematic approach to troubleshooting plumbing problems and a list of basic tools needed for making repairs. The following chapters show the inner parts of faucets and drains, along with illustrated step-by-step instructions that will help you make repairs easily. The book includes information on toilets, garbage disposals, and tub and shower plumbing. It also shows you how to work with pipe.

Most of the repairs in the book can be accomplished quickly and inexpensively. Making your own repairs can be personally satisfying and can save you a service call from a plumber, who might be too busy to get to your home for several days.

Today's plumbing materials and equipment are designed to make repairs or replacements easier for the homeowner as well as the professional. These advances have greatly reduced the amount of physical effort required for plumbing work and have made the repair techniques easy to master. In the past, plumbing materials were made of lead, iron, galvanized steel, and brass. Today they are mostly copper and plastic.

Home plumbing system.

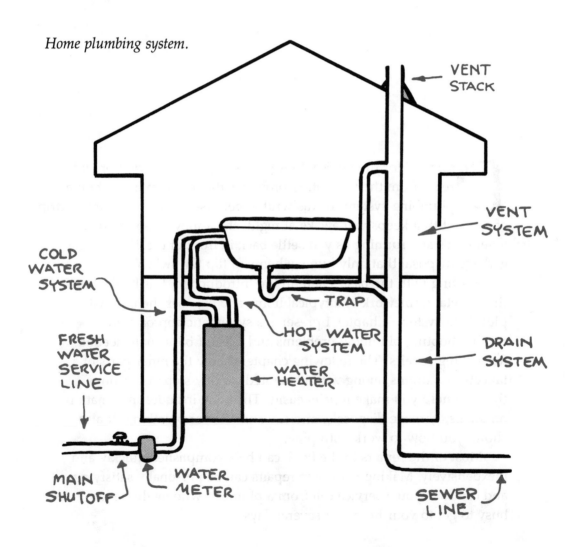

The major part of the plumbing system is hidden within the walls and under the floors. Normally we only see the chrome faucets, porcelain fixtures, and stainless steel sinks. Although these come in a variety of shapes and designs, the inner workings of plumbing systems are pretty much the same in all homes. Supply lines, under as much as 40 pounds of pressure per square inch, deliver fresh water to various locations throughout the house. Waste water, under normal atmospheric pressure, is drained off by gravity to main sewer lines or, in rural areas, to septic tanks on the property.

Two important components in the waste system are traps and vent stacks. The *trap*, which is beneath each sink, tub, or shower in the house, is a U-shaped pipe that stays full of water all the time. The water forms a seal in the waste line and prevents odors and combustible gases from entering the home.

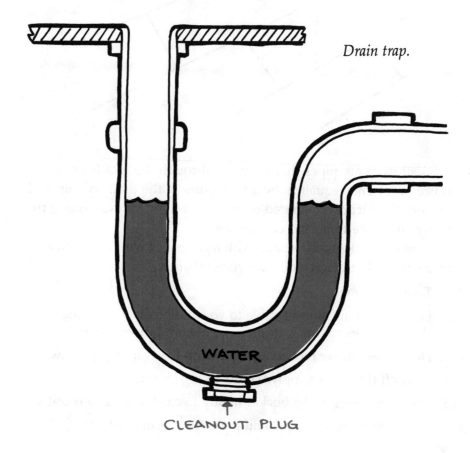

Drain trap.

WATER

CLEANOUT PLUG

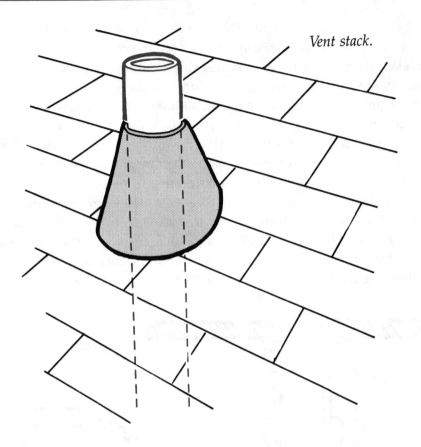

Vent stack.

Vent stacks are pipes that protrude through the roof from the waste lines. They equalize the air pressure in the drain system and prevent the suction generated by flowing water from siphoning the water out of the traps and commodes.

You can make most repairs with a couple of wrenches and a screwdriver, but before you start remember to:

1. Take your time.
2. Locate the main shutoff valve to your home, as well as the shutoff valves to sinks, clothes washer, and dishwasher.
3. Do not use power tools or electric drop lights in damp areas.
4. Shut off the water supply before taking faucets apart.
5. Have a few rags and a bucket handy to catch any spilled water.
6. Cover the drain to keep small parts from being lost.

CHAPTER ONE

Basic Troubleshooting & Tools

Plumbing systems have just two basic areas: the high-pressure side that delivers fresh water throughout the home, and the low-pressure side that uses gravity to carry wastewater away. Typically, fresh water enters the house from a meter on the street side of the house. The supply pipe is usually 3/4 inch or larger and has a *shutoff valve* near the meter or just inside the wall where the pipe enters the house. The supply pipe then feeds branch runs of smaller pipes, usually 1/2 inch in diameter, that deliver water to the water heater and other sections of the system. Except for the shutoff valves, these pipes are buried in the ground or hidden in the walls until they arrive at the various fixtures. There, a shutoff valve is normally installed and the pipe diameter is reduced again. The pipe then supplies water to the fixture. Wastewater goes down a drain, then travels through a trap and into the main sewer line leading from the house.

If you know where the shutoff valves are, you can quickly handle emergencies such as a burst pipe or washer hose. Here are a few pointers for handling other basic plumbing problems:

- When small objects such as rings disappear down the drain, don't run water in the sink. Get a bucket, place it under the trap beneath the sink, and check the trap.

- If a sink won't drain or a toilet becomes blocked, don't run more water in the sink or flush the toilet. Use a plunger to remove the blockage, then run fresh water.

- If an electrical appliance such as a clothes washer, dishwasher, or garbage disposal is leaking, turn off the power before touching the appliance or attempting any repairs. Unplug the appliance if you can stay out of the water, or turn off the power at the *electrical panel*.

- If a basement becomes flooded or an electrical outlet is under water, don't enter the room. The first thing to do is turn off the power at the electrical panel. Then, shut off the water at the *main valve*.

- If sewage odors occur, run water in the sinks to make sure the traps are full of water.

While today's materials make plumbing easier to do, you do need to work carefully and have the proper tools. If you have a job that requires an expensive tool—one you probably won't need often—you can usually rent it at a tool-rental store or from your plumbing supply dealer where you buy parts. Most plumbing repairs can be handled with basic tools along with the following plumbing tools shown on the next few pages.

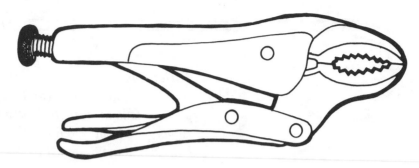

Locking pliers   *Locking pliers provide an adjustable, viselike grip that, once in place, holds a fitting by itself.*

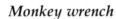

Monkey wrench
A monkey wrench is similar to a pipe wrench except that its smooth jaws are less likely to scratch chrome fittings. A handy size for home use is one with a 10- or 12-inch handle.

Pipe wrench   *A pipe wrench has toothed jaws where the top adjustable jaw pivots. The jaws tighten their grip as pressure is applied to the handle, which keeps them from slipping on pipes. They are normally used in pairs, with one wrench on the pipe and the other wrench on the fitting. The toothed jaws will damage chrome fittings.*

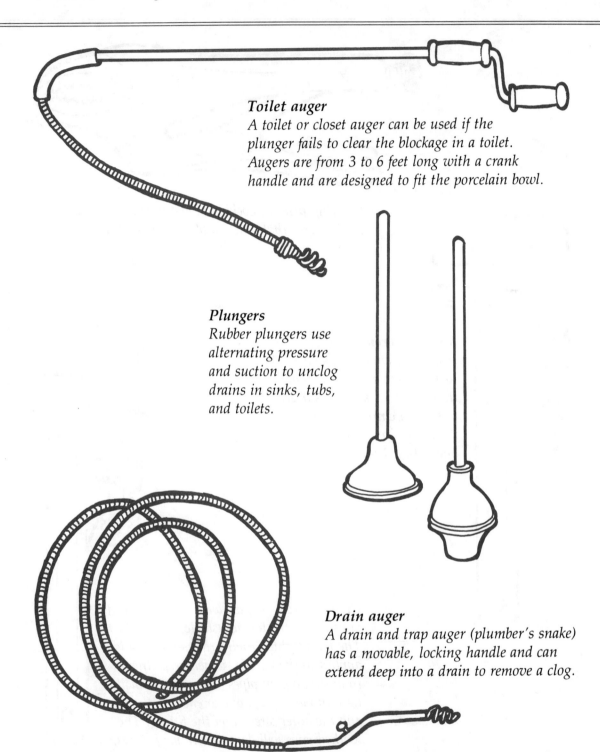

Toilet auger
A toilet or closet auger can be used if the plunger fails to clear the blockage in a toilet. Augers are from 3 to 6 feet long with a crank handle and are designed to fit the porcelain bowl.

Plungers
Rubber plungers use alternating pressure and suction to unclog drains in sinks, tubs, and toilets.

Drain auger
A drain and trap auger (plumber's snake) has a movable, locking handle and can extend deep into a drain to remove a clog.

Wire brush
A wire cleaning brush is used to scour the inside of copper fittings to prepare them for soldering.

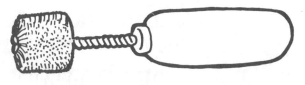

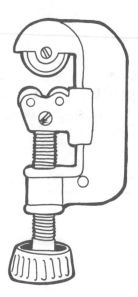

Tube cutter
A tube cutter cuts copper and plastic tubing and has a reamer that swings out to deburr the cut end.

Faucet-seat dresser
A faucet-seat dresser, or seat dressing tool, comes with different-sized guides and cutting tips. It is designed to smooth worn or damaged faucets that can't be removed with a seat wrench. These tools can be expensive—try renting instead of buying.

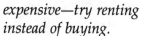

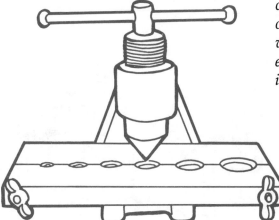

Flaring tool
A flaring tool is used to flare the end of a tube so that it can be attached to flared fittings.

Tube bender   *A tube bender is a coiled, springlike tool that allows you to bend tubing without kinking it.*

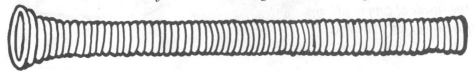

Basin wrench   *A basin wrench is a valuable tool that lets you get to hard-to-reach nuts hidden under bathroom and kitchen sinks. The head swivels, allowing the wrench to work at all angles.*

Seat wrench

A seat wrench has a square end and a hexagonal end and is used to remove and install faucet seats. The right-angle tool shown can be turned by hand. A straight tool must be turned with a wrench.

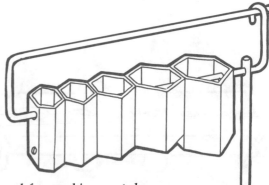

Plumber's sockets
Socket wrenches are used for working on tub and shower faucets that are recessed in the walls. They are normally sold in sets of five sockets and a bar handle.

Pipe tape
*Teflon pipe tape can be
wrapped around male threads to
provide watertight seals where
threaded pipe enters fittings.*

Flux
*Flux (noncorrosive) is available
in paste and liquid form.
It is used to clean copper and
help the solder flow.*

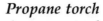

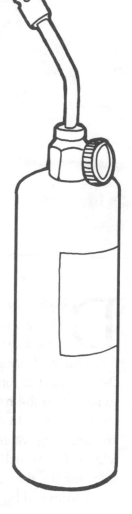

Penetrating oil
*Penetrating oil will help
loosen corroded fittings.*

Propane torch
*A propane torch is
used to heat copper
tubing for soldering.*

Plumbing solder
*Plumbing solder (not electrical)
is used to join fittings to copper pipe.
Some plumbing codes require a low-lead
(90/10 percent tin/lead) solder.*

CHAPTER TWO

Repairing Faucets

D espite the fact that faucets come in many different sizes and shapes, they can be divided into two basic types: stem faucets and single-lever faucets. *Stem faucets* are made up of these internal parts: a threaded shaft (the *stem*), a packing washer or O-ring near the top of the stem, and a washer at the bottom of the stem. When the handle is turned on, the stem rotates. The threads cause the stem to rise, moving the washer away from the *faucet seat* and allowing water to flow. When the handle is turned off, the stem rotates downward, pressing the washer against the faucet seat and stopping the flow of water. The *packing washer* or the O-ring prevents water from leaking around the handle when the water is on.

Tools & Materials

☐ Knife or small screwdriver
☐ Pliers
☐ Adjustable wrench
☐ Washers, screws, and nuts
☐ Flashlight
☐ Hex wrench
☐ Faucet seat wrench
☐ Seat dressing tool
☐ Petroleum jelly
☐ Needle-nose pliers
☐ Replacement parts as needed

When a stem faucet drips, the problem is usually caused by a worn washer or faucet seat. If water leaks from the handle, the packing washer or O-ring is probably worn.

A two-handled stem faucet.

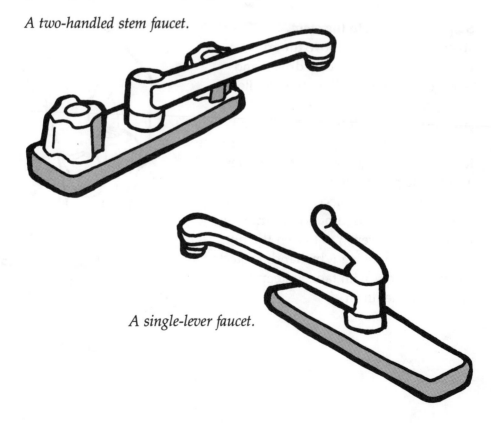

A single-lever faucet.

Step 2-1. Finding the leak.
To find out which handle is faulty, shut off one of the valves below the sink. If the drip stops, the problem is in that side of the faucet. If the drip continues, the other handle needs repair. Before starting to work, turn off the water supply and open the faucet. Plug the drain with a rag or stopper to keep small parts from being lost.

Step 2-2. Getting to the stem.
To get to the stem, remove the trim cap with a knife or small screwdriver, and remove the screw holding the handle to the stem. Lift off the handle. If it is stubborn, apply a little penetrating oil and rock the handle gently upward. If it still won't budge, wait a few minutes and let the penetrating oil do its work. The stem is held in place with a *locknut*, or on older models, a packing nut. Use an adjustable wrench to loosen the nut, then finish removing it by hand. Protect the packing nut with tape to keep from scratching the finish.

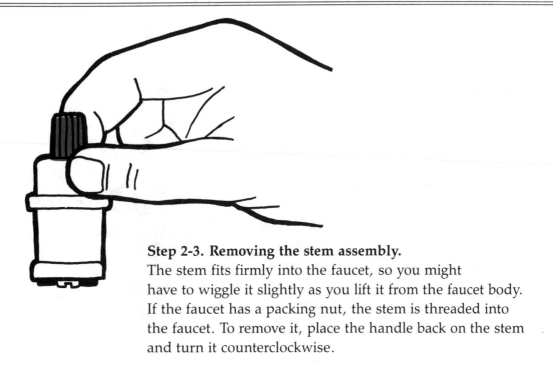

Step 2-3. Removing the stem assembly.
The stem fits firmly into the faucet, so you might
have to wiggle it slightly as you lift it from the faucet body.
If the faucet has a packing nut, the stem is threaded into
the faucet. To remove it, place the handle back on the stem
and turn it counterclockwise.

Step 2-4. Replacing the washer on a standard stem.
To replace the washer on a standard stem, remove the retaining screw
and pry out the old washer with the tip of a knife or small screwdriver.
If the screw head is badly corroded, you might have to use pliers
to loosen it. Install the new washer. If it's a tapering washer, place
the tapered side facing down toward the faucet seat. The top of the
washer should fit snugly into the stem cup. Install a new retaining
screw, and tighten it until it begins to compress the washer, holding
the washer firmly inside the cup.

Step 2-5.

Replacing a washer on a reverse-pressure stem.
To replace a washer on a reverse-pressure stem,
use an adjustable wrench to remove the nut on
the bottom of the stem. Remove the nut-washer,
washer retainer, and the stem washer. Install
the new stem washer with the tapered side up
toward the faucet seat. Place the washer on
the threaded end of the stem followed by
the washer retainer, nut washer, and nut.
Tightening the nut completes the assembly.

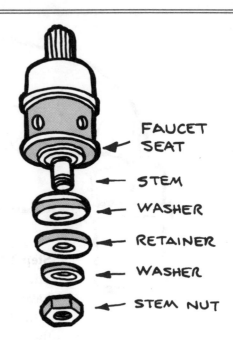

FAUCET SEAT
STEM
WASHER
RETAINER
WASHER
STEM NUT

Step 2-6.

Replacing a hat-shaped diaphragm.
To replace a hat-shaped diaphragm, just remove
the old diaphragm by hand and press a new one
over the rounded lip on the end of the stem.

Step 2-7. Checking the faucet seat.

If the faucet continues to drip after replacing the washer, the problem is probably with the faucet seat. Remove the stem assembly and examine the faucet seat. Run your finger over the seat's surface. The seat should be smooth. Check it with a flashlight. You might have to soak up water over the seat with a small piece of rag or paper towel.

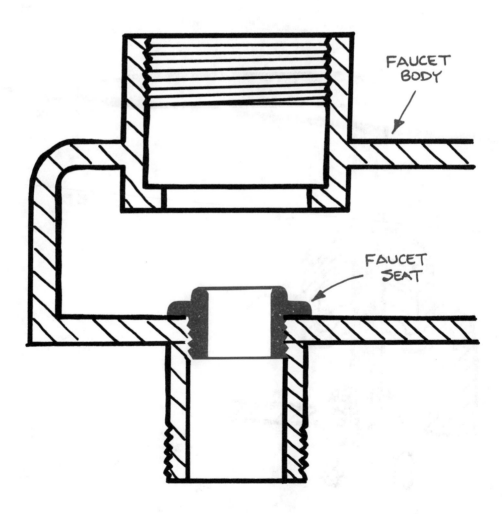

FAUCET BODY

FAUCET SEAT

Step 2-8. Replacing the faucet seat.

If you find any cuts or pits in the faucet seat, remove it
with a *hex wrench* or the hexagonal end of a faucet seat wrench,
turning the old seat counterclockwise. If the seat is frozen in place,
apply a little penetrating oil and wait a while. Start the new seat
by hand and tighten it with the seat wrench. In some faucets,
the seat is part of the faucet body and cannot be removed.
You can grind these seats smooth with a seat dressing tool.

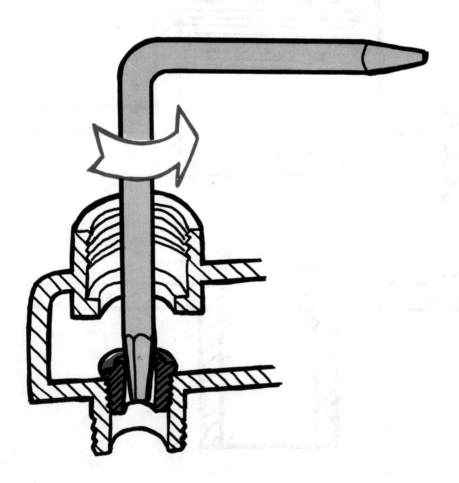

Step 2-9. Dressing the seat.

To smooth a worn faucet seat, rent or buy a seat dressing tool. They come with several sizes of cutters and seat guides. Select the largest cutter that fits the faucet seat and a guide that fits the seat hole. With the cutter and guide in place, screw the cone down snugly into the faucet body. Now turn the knob on the tool a few smooth, steady turns. You don't need to press down on the tool much—the seat is made of soft brass and cuts easily. After a few turns, the knob will be easy to turn. The seat should now be dressed. Remove the tool and wipe away the filings with a damp rag. Reassemble the faucet and check it for leaks. If it still leaks, repeat the seat-dressing process. If dressing the seat twice fails to stop the leak, you might have to replace the faucet.

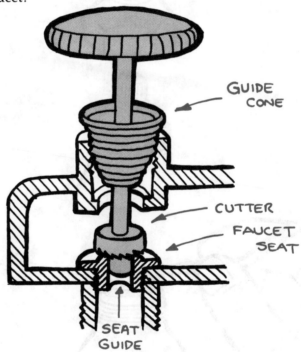

Sometimes water will seep up near the handle of a faucet and will leak from around the top of the faucet stem. The cure for this problem depends on the type of faucet. If the faucet is installed with a packing nut, the packing washer or *packing material* probably needs replacing. If the faucet has a locknut, the O-ring is probably bad.

Step 2-10. Fixing a faucet with a packing nut.

If a faucet with a packing nut has a stem leak, first try gently tightening the packing nut. If this fails to stop the leak, turn off the water, remove the nut, and replace the packing washer. If the stem has packing material, add a few turns of new packing string or pipe tape to the old packing. Screw the packing nut back on. It will compress the packing. Don't overtighten the packing nut. Install the handle and check for leaks.

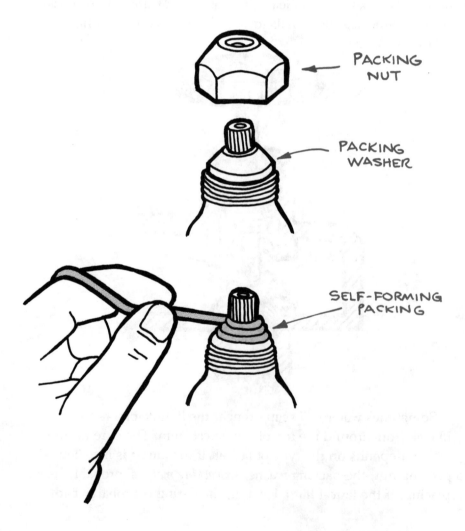

PACKING NUT

PACKING WASHER

SELF-FORMING PACKING

Step 2-11. Fixing a faucet with an O-ring.

If the faucet has an O-ring, turn off the water and remove the stem assembly. Press the O-ring from the sides so that part of it comes out of the O-ring groove. Remove the O-ring and take it with you to buy a new one. You need an exact replacement. Discard the old one so it won't accidentally be reinstalled. Lubricate the new O-ring with petroleum jelly, slip it on the stem, and reassemble the faucet.

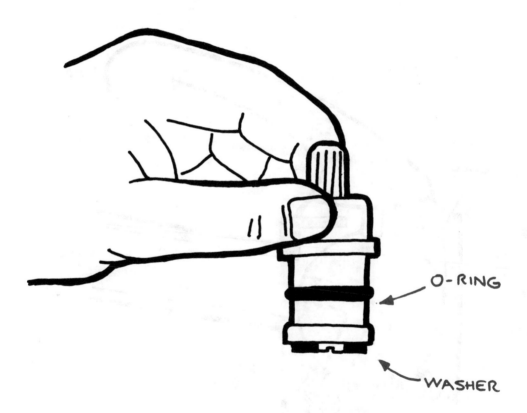

Single-lever faucets come in variations of three basic models: ball faucet, sleeve-cartridge faucet, and ceramic-disc cartridge faucet. You can easily make repairs from prepackaged repair kits or by installing a new cartridge.

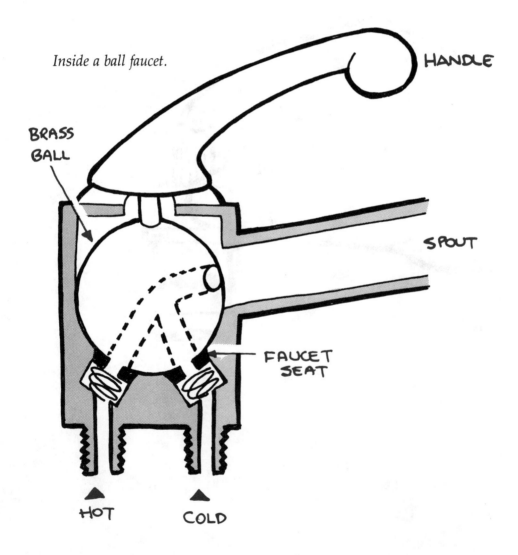

Inside a ball faucet.

HANDLE

BRASS BALL

SPOUT

FAUCET SEAT

HOT

COLD

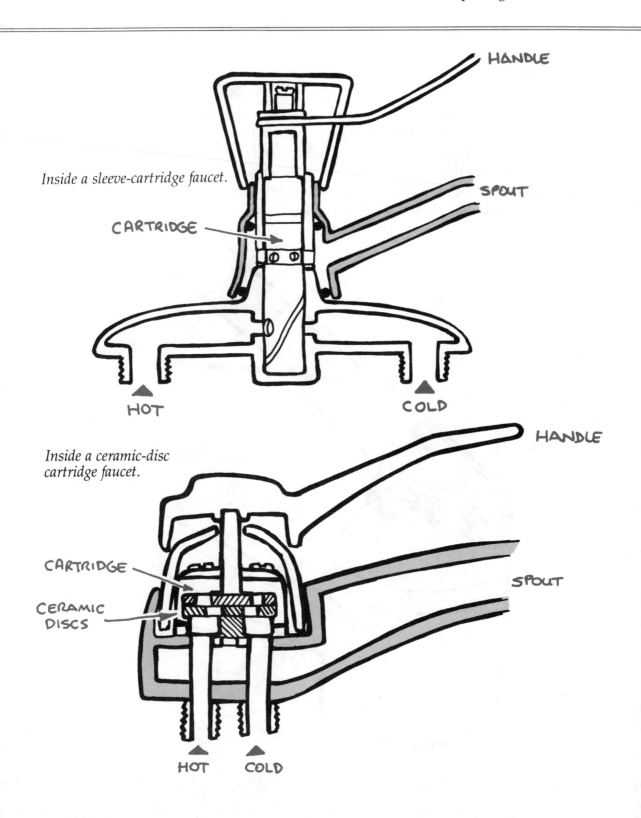

HANDLE

Inside a sleeve-cartridge faucet.

CARTRIDGE

SPOUT

HOT

COLD

HANDLE

Inside a ceramic-disc cartridge faucet.

CARTRIDGE

CERAMIC DISCS

SPOUT

HOT

COLD

Step 2-12. Tightening the adjusting ring in a ball faucet.
To service a ball faucet, loosen the *setscrew* at the base of the handle, and remove the handle. Below the handle, you will see a protective cap with an adjusting ring. Sometimes a dripping faucet can be fixed by tightening this ring. Place the edge of a dinner knife across the gaps in the ring and turn it clockwise. Don't overtighten; the ball should move easily with the handle removed.

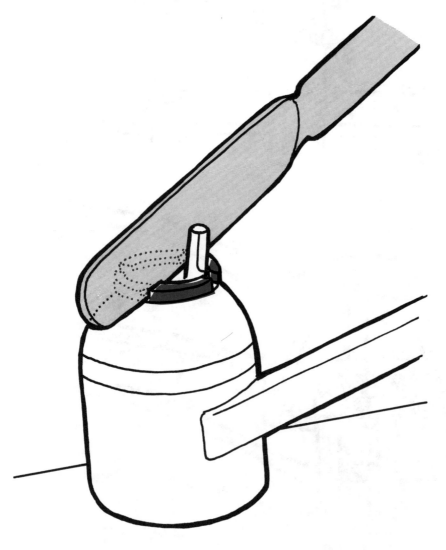

Step 2-13. Disassembling the faucet.
If tightening the ring fails to stop
the leak, close both shutoff valves
beneath the sink and open the
faucet. Remove the handle.
Unscrew and lift off the cap,
plastic cam, cam washer, and
rotating ball. Use a hex wrench
to loosen the setscrew. Gently
wiggle the spout and pull
it straight up.

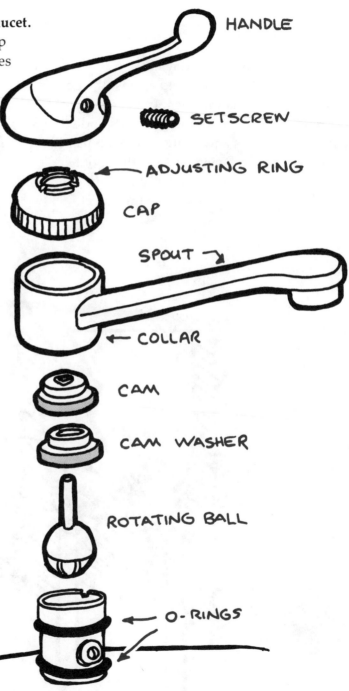

HANDLE

SETSCREW

ADJUSTING RING

CAP

SPOUT

COLLAR

CAM

CAM WASHER

ROTATING BALL

O-RINGS

Step 2-14.
Replacing seats and O-rings.
Rubber faucet seats are held against the bottom
of the ball by small springs. Use the point of a
screwdriver to remove the two seats and springs.
Install new seats and springs from a repair kit,
and replace the O-rings. Lower the spout
straight down over the collar to prevent damage
to the O-rings and reassemble the faucet.

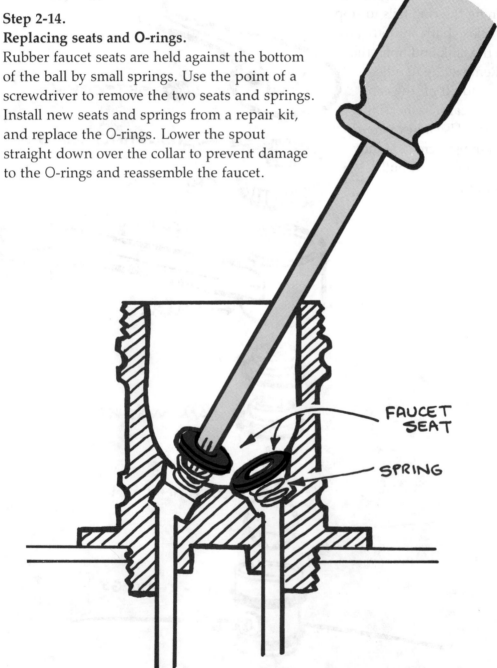

FAUCET
SEAT

SPRING

Step 2-15. Repairing a ceramic-disc cartridge faucet.

To service a ceramic-disc faucet, first close both shutoff valves beneath the sink and open the faucet. Use a hex wrench to loosen the setscrew at the base of the handle. Some screws are hidden behind a decorative button. Pry the button off with a small screwdriver. Remove the handle. Beneath the handle is a cap that could be screwed to the faucet body or held in place by a plastic adapter. Unscrew the cap or pry it off.

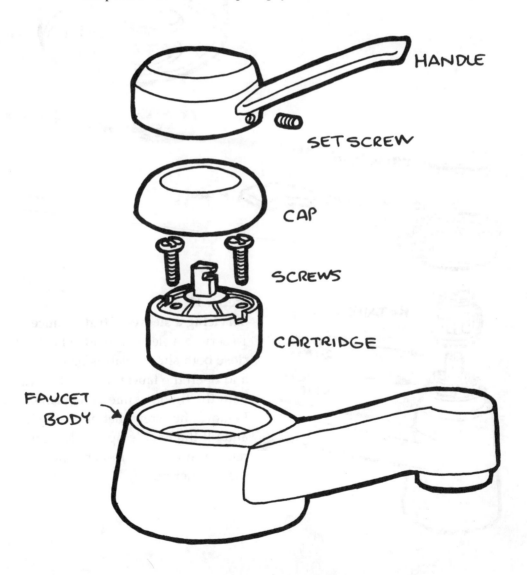

Step 2-16. Checking the cartridge.
Remove the two or three screws holding the cartridge
in place and lift out the cartridge. Check the
cartridge for cracks or pits and replace it
if necessary. Install new seals and align
the cartridge in the faucet body so that
the three holes line up. Install the
cartridge screws but don't overtighten.
Reassemble the faucet.

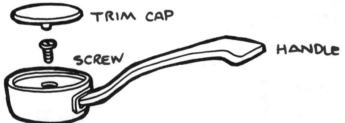

Step 2-17.
Servicing a sleeve-cartridge faucet.
To service a sleeve-cartridge faucet, first
close both shutoff valves beneath the sink
and open the faucet. Pry off the trim cover
with the tip of a knife or a small screwdriver.
Remove the screw that holds the handle
and tilt the handle up to release it from the
retainer nut. Use slip-joint pliers to remove
the retainer nut.

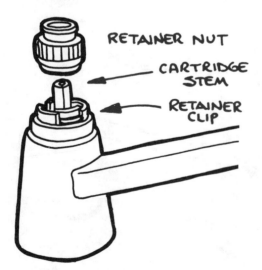

Step 2-18. Removing the clip.
Find the U-shaped clip that holds in the cartridge.
Use the tip of a screwdriver or needle-nose pliers to pull out the clip.

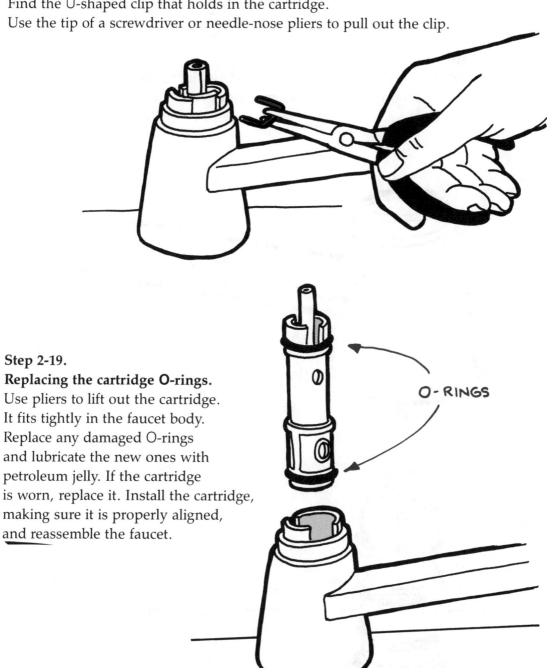

Step 2-19.
Replacing the cartridge O-rings.
Use pliers to lift out the cartridge.
It fits tightly in the faucet body.
Replace any damaged O-rings
and lubricate the new ones with
petroleum jelly. If the cartridge
is worn, replace it. Install the cartridge,
making sure it is properly aligned,
and reassemble the faucet.

O-RINGS

Step 2-20. Replacing spout O-rings.

To replace spout O-rings, remove the retainer nut and lift off the spout. Replace the O-rings, lubricating the new ones with petroleum jelly.

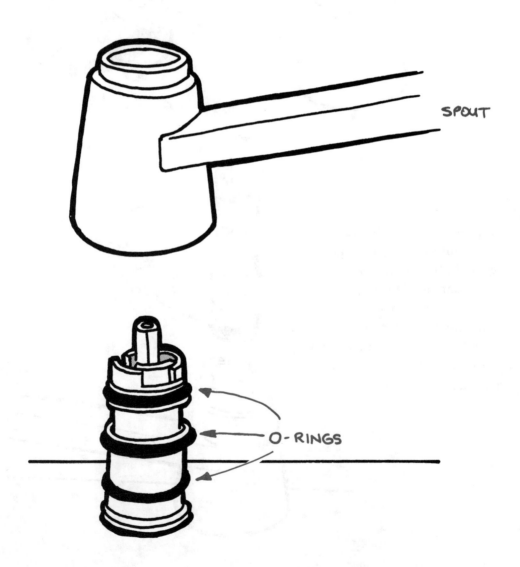

CHAPTER THREE

Replacing Faucets

Replacing an old faucet is often put off because the job appears to be too difficult or expensive. Actually, replacement is very easy and new faucets are not expensive. The biggest problem is the cramped work space beneath the sink. First remove all items in the storage area and spread a few newspapers under the sink. Have a bucket ready to catch any excess water. Use a basin wrench to get to the fittings and have an adjustable wrench handy.

Tools & Materials

- ☐ Adjustable wrench
- ☐ Basin wrench
- ☐ Putty knife
- ☐ Tape measure or ruler
- ☐ Faucet
- ☐ Plumber's putty (optional)
- ☐ Replacement parts as needed

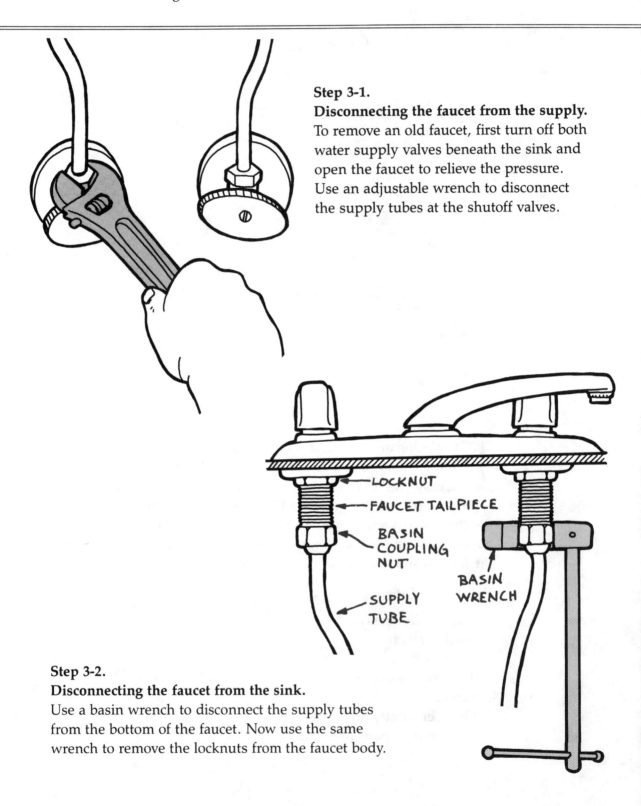

Step 3-1.
Disconnecting the faucet from the supply.
To remove an old faucet, first turn off both
water supply valves beneath the sink and
open the faucet to relieve the pressure.
Use an adjustable wrench to disconnect
the supply tubes at the shutoff valves.

LOCKNUT

FAUCET TAILPIECE

BASIN
COUPLING
NUT

BASIN
WRENCH

SUPPLY
TUBE

Step 3-2.
Disconnecting the faucet from the sink.
Use a basin wrench to disconnect the supply tubes
from the bottom of the faucet. Now use the same
wrench to remove the locknuts from the faucet body.

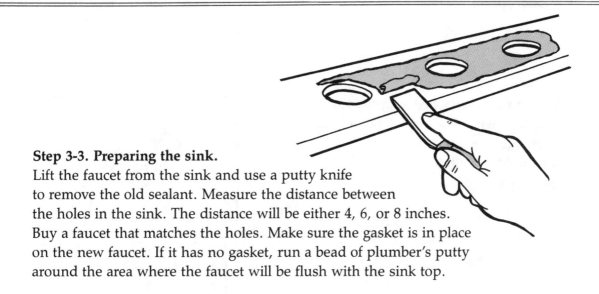

Step 3-3. Preparing the sink.

Lift the faucet from the sink and use a putty knife
to remove the old sealant. Measure the distance between
the holes in the sink. The distance will be either 4, 6, or 8 inches.
Buy a faucet that matches the holes. Make sure the gasket is in place
on the new faucet. If it has no gasket, run a bead of plumber's putty
around the area where the faucet will be flush with the sink top.

Step 3-4. Installing the new faucet.

Work the faucet water-supply tubes
through the center hole in the sink.
Install a washer and nut on each
threaded stud on the bottom
of the faucet. Tighten them
with the basin wrench or
by hand if they are plastic.

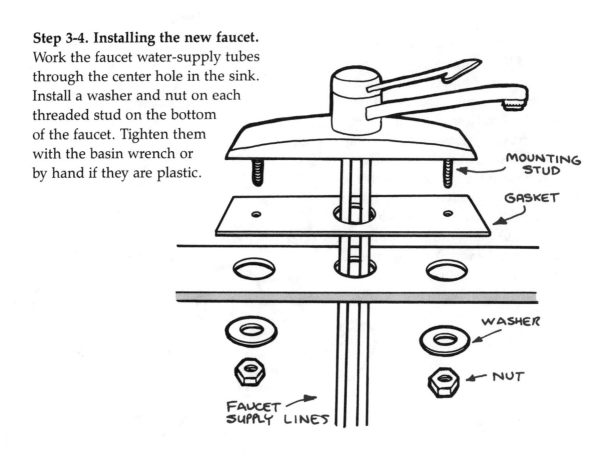

MOUNTING STUD

GASKET

WASHER

NUT

FAUCET SUPPLY LINES

Step 3-5.
Connecting the attached supply tubes.
Using a tube bender, carefully bend the
supply tubes on the faucet so that they line up
with the fittings on the shutoff valve.

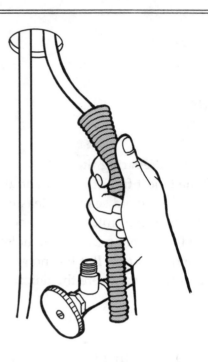

Step 3-6.
Tightening the compression nuts.
First, slide a compression nut and ring on the
free end of the supply tube. Then push
the end of the tube into the nipple of
the shutoff valve as far as it will go.
Slide the compression ring down to
the tapered opening in the valve.
Next, thread the nut on the valve as
far as you can by hand, then tighten
a quarter turn with an adjustable
wrench. Connect the other supply
tube the same way. You might need
to use an adapter to attach the
supply tube to the shutoff valve.

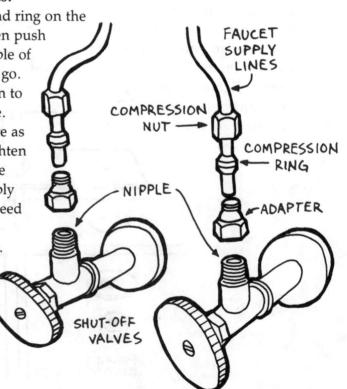

FAUCET
SUPPLY
LINES

COMPRESSION
NUT →

COMPRESSION
← RING

NIPPLE

ADAPTER

SHUT-OFF
VALVES

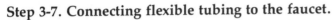

Step 3-7. Connecting flexible tubing to the faucet.
To install a faucet that has no attached supply tubes, use flexible supply tubes, which come in lengths up to 36 inches. Place the washer inside the $1/2$-inch nut on the end of the flexible tube and thread the nut onto the bottom of the faucet. Tighten it with the basin wrench. Connect the other flexible tube the same way.

Step 3-8.
Connecting flexible tubing to the water supply.
Thread the nut on the other end of the tube to the outlet on the shutoff valve. Screw it on by hand, then tighten it a quarter turn with an adjustable wrench. Connect the other flexible tube the same way. Turn on the water and check for leaks.

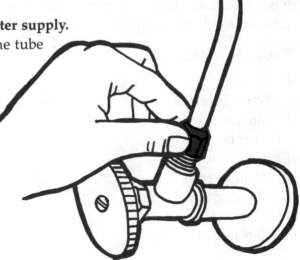

CHAPTER FOUR

Repairing Sink Sprays

P roblems with sink sprays are usually limited to low water flow, a leaky spray head, or a defective diverter valve. Often, you can solve these problems with a simple cleaning, so check it out first. Then, if you need any parts—usually O-rings and washers —take the old ones with you when you buy the replacements.

Tools & Materials

- ☐ Knife
- ☐ Screwdriver
- ☐ Vinegar
- ☐ Toothbrush
- ☐ Needle-nose pliers
- ☐ Basin wrench
- ☐ Masking tape
- ☐ Pliers
- ☐ Replacement parts as needed

Step 4-1. Cleaning sprayer parts.

To clean the spray head, first unscrew the spray head assembly.
Then, holding the sprayer in the sink, turn on the faucet and press
the sprayer handle to flush out the head. On some sprayers, the
assembly is held in place with a screw. Use the tip of a knife to pry
off the screw cover. Remove the screw and any parts it held. Keep
them in the order that they were removed. Clean the parts by
soaking them in vinegar and scrubbing them with an old toothbrush.
Replace the washers and reassemble the spray head.

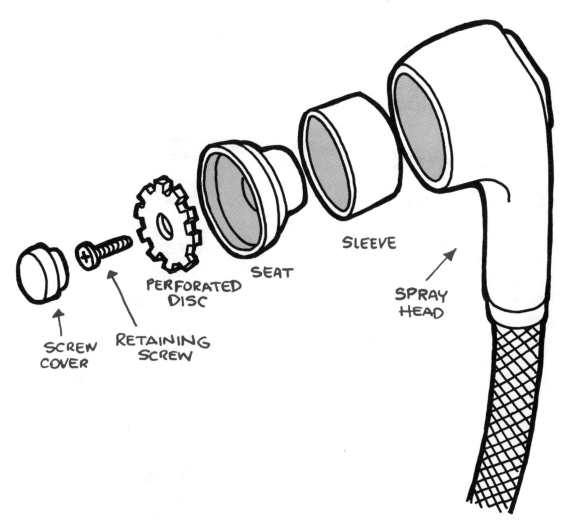

SLEEVE

SEAT

PERFORATED
DISC

SPRAY
HEAD

SCREW
COVER

RETAINING
SCREW

SPRAY HEAD

WASHER

PLASTIC RING

RETAINING CLIP

COUPLING

GROOVE FOR RETAINING CLIP

HOSE

Step 4-2. Removing the spray hose.

To replace the spray hose, make sure the sprayer is shut off, then unscrew the coupling from the spray head. You should find a washer that fits inside the spray head. Replace it if it is worn. Remove the plastic ring over the steel retaining clip and pull out the retaining clip with needle-nose pliers. Slide the coupling from the hose. Use a basin wrench to loosen the hex nut connecting the other end of the hose to the bottom of the faucet. Unscrew it by hand.

Step 4-3. Installing a new hose.

Push the other end of the new hose up through the hole in the sink. Slide the coupling over the end and install the retaining clip, plastic ring, and washer. Reattach the spray head. Then connect the new hose to the bottom of the faucet.

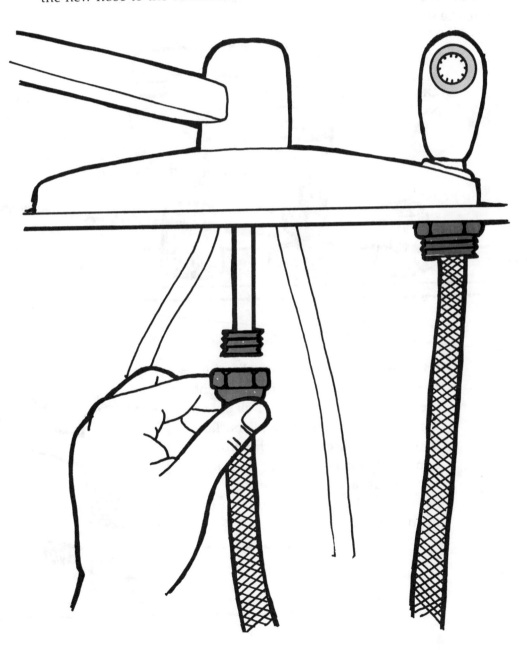

Step 4-4. Repairing a diverter valve.

To repair a *diverter valve*, first close both shutoff valves beneath the sink and take the faucet apart down to removing the spout. If the faucet has two handles, unscrew the spout nut and remove the diverter valve. Some valves can be removed by hand, others must be screwed out.

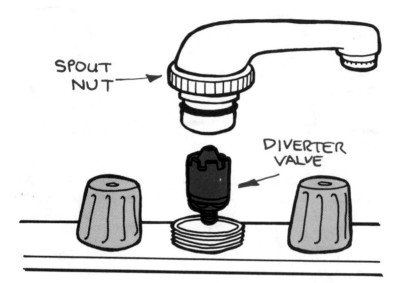

SPOUT NUT

DIVERTER VALVE

If the faucet has only one handle, the diverter valve might fit horizontally into the front of the faucet base. Pull out the valve with needle-nose pliers. Take it to another faucet and wash it to remove any foreign particles. Replace any O-rings, and reassemble the faucet. If problems continue, replace the diverter valve.

DIVERTER VALVE

Step 4-5. Cleaning the aerator.

To clean the *aerator*, protect the chrome finish with masking tape and use pliers to unscrew the aerator from the spout. Place the parts to one side in the order of their removal. Clean the screen by soaking it in vinegar and scrubbing it with an old toothbrush. Replace the washer if it is worn and reassemble the aerator. Thread it in place by hand and tighten a quarter turn with pliers.

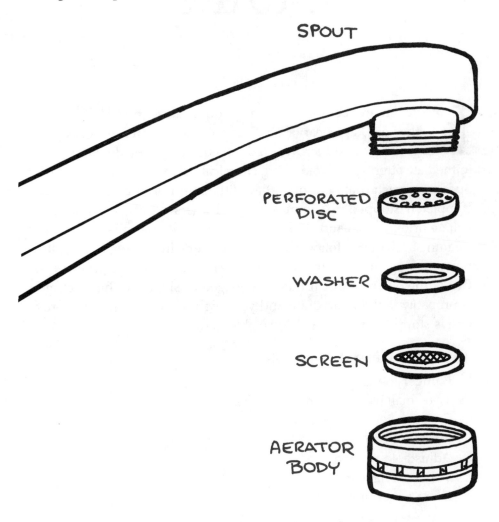

SPOUT

PERFORATED DISC

WASHER

SCREEN

AERATOR BODY

CHAPTER FIVE

Unclogging Drains

K itchen and bathroom drains seldom cause any problems if they are kept clear of obstructions such as grease, coffee grounds, and hair. When drains do clog, they demand immediate attention. Avoid using chemical drain cleaners; they might open a sluggish drain but often have little effect on drains that are completely stopped up. Because these cleaners are caustic and can irritate or burn eyes and skin on contact, reserve their use for periodic cleaning and always follow the manufacturer's instructions carefully. Before taking anything apart, try to determine where the problem is. Check the other drains. If they are clogged or sluggish, the blockage is probably in the main drain and you might need a plumber. If only one is stopped up, you should be able to fix it.

Tools & Materials
- Plunger
- Two small blocks wood
- C-clamp
- Bucket or pan
- Adjustable wrench
- Wire coat hanger
- Drain auger (if necessary)

Step 5-1. Plugging the openings.

To use a plunger on a kitchen sink, remove the sink strainer
and stuff a wet rag into the overflow opening. If it is a double sink,
pack wet rags in one of the drain openings. You might need someone
to hold the rags in place while you work the plunger.

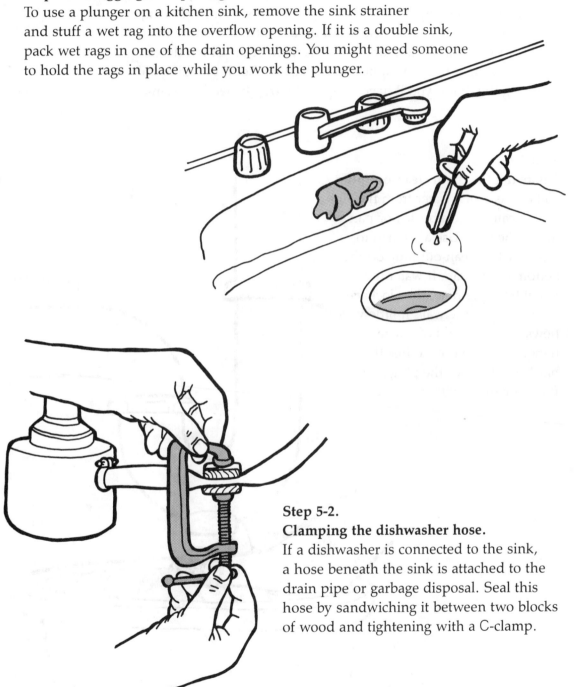

Step 5-2.
Clamping the dishwasher hose.

If a dishwasher is connected to the sink,
a hose beneath the sink is attached to the
drain pipe or garbage disposal. Seal this
hose by sandwiching it between two blocks
of wood and tightening with a C-clamp.

Fill the sink about half full with water. Place the plunger directly over the drain opening. Push the plunger down smoothly, forcing water against the blockage. Then pull up abruptly, loosening the clog from the pipe. Pump the plunger in this manner about ten times, abruptly lifting it from the water on the last stroke. If plunging fails to unclog the drain, you'll have to open the trap beneath the sink.

Step 5-3.
Removing the drain clean-out plug.
Bail out as much water from the sink as you can. Place a bucket or pan under the trap. Use a wrench to unscrew the clean-out plug on the bottom of the trap. If water flows freely from the hole, the blockage is probably in the wall. If little water flows, stick the end of a wire coat hanger into the hole to free the blockage. Replace the plug and flush the drain with hot water.

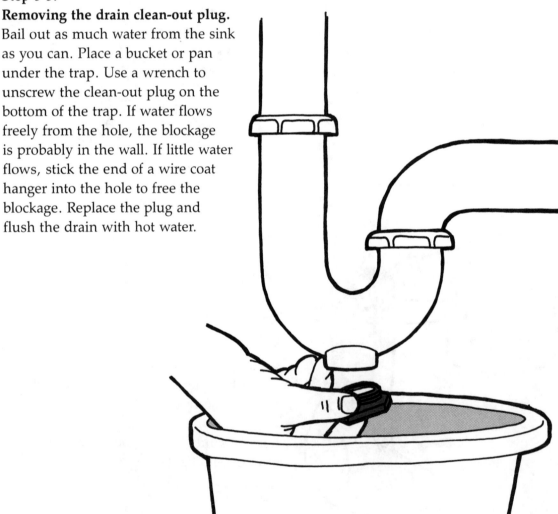

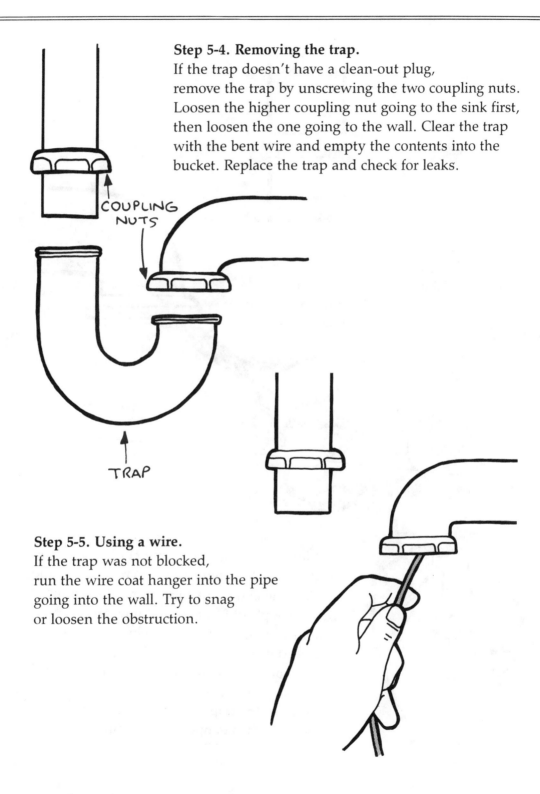

Step 5-4. Removing the trap.
If the trap doesn't have a clean-out plug,
remove the trap by unscrewing the two coupling nuts.
Loosen the higher coupling nut going to the sink first,
then loosen the one going to the wall. Clear the trap
with the bent wire and empty the contents into the
bucket. Replace the trap and check for leaks.

COUPLING NUTS

TRAP

Step 5-5. Using a wire.
If the trap was not blocked,
run the wire coat hanger into the pipe
going into the wall. Try to snag
or loosen the obstruction.

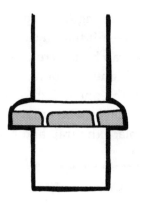

Step 5-6. Using a drain auger.

If you still can't reach the clog, you need a drain auger. An *auger* is a flexible steel cable with a movable handle. Feed the end of the cable into the drain pipe. Allow about 2 feet of slack for the handle.

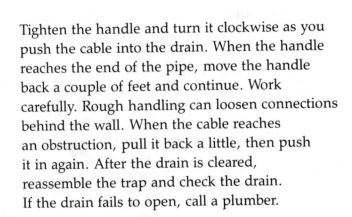

Tighten the handle and turn it clockwise as you push the cable into the drain. When the handle reaches the end of the pipe, move the handle back a couple of feet and continue. Work carefully. Rough handling can loosen connections behind the wall. When the cable reaches an obstruction, pull it back a little, then push it in again. After the drain is cleared, reassemble the trap and check the drain. If the drain fails to open, call a plumber.

CHAPTER SIX

Replacing Sink Strainers & Pop-up Drains

S trainers are made to keep utensils from falling into the drain. They sometimes need attention because of leaks, or they might become discolored or worn and need replacing. Pop-up drains in bathroom sinks are much handier than the old rubber stoppers, but they seldom close tight enough to make a good seal. They can, however, be easily adjusted or taken apart for cleaning.

Tools & Materials

- ☐ Adjustable wrench
- ☐ Wooden dowel
- ☐ Hammer
- ☐ Pipe wrench
- ☐ Pliers
- ☐ Screwdriver
- ☐ Putty knife
- ☐ Plumber's putty
- ☐ Stiff brush
- ☐ O-rings
- ☐ Replacement parts as needed

Strainers are fastened to the sink by two different methods. One kind is held in place by a locknut, while the other is fastened by a retainer tightened by three screws.

Two types of strainers.

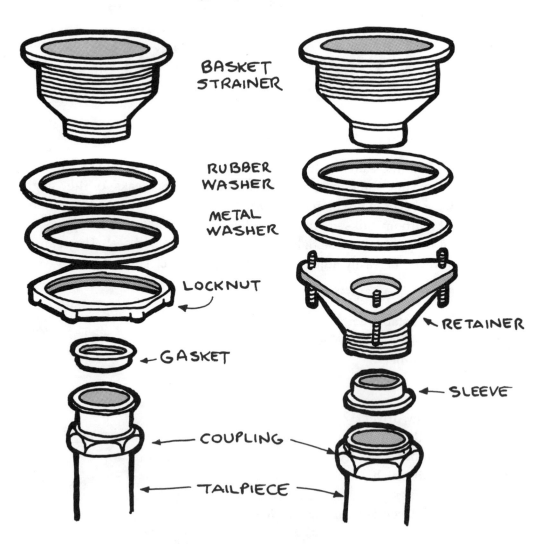

BASKET STRAINER

RUBBER WASHER

METAL WASHER

LOCKNUT

GASKET

RETAINER

SLEEVE

COUPLING

TAILPIECE

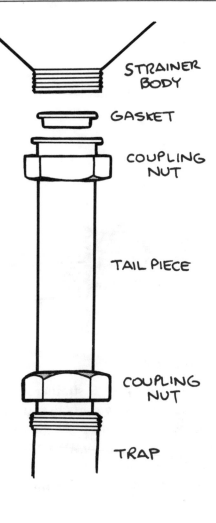

Step 6-1. Disconnecting the tailpiece.
To remove the strainer, use a wrench to
unscrew the two *coupling nuts* on the *tailpiece*.
Let the tailpiece slide down into the trap and
out of the way. Remove the locknut holding
the strainer to the sink.

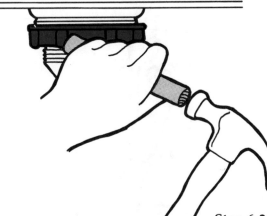

Step 6-2. Removing the large locknut.
This type of nut is a large metal ring with
ridges. To loosen it, place the end of a wooden
dowel or some other blunt rod against the
ridges and tap the nut loose with a hammer.

Step 6-3. Removing the smaller locknut.
You can remove this smaller locknut with a wrench.

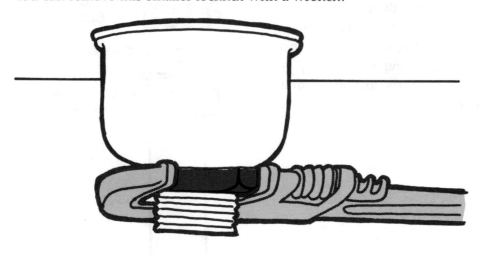

Step 6-4. Holding the strainer.
If the strainer body starts to turn as you
unscrew the locknut, place the handles of a pair
of pliers in the strainer. With your free hand,
hold the pliers steady with the blade of a long
screwdriver while you turn the locknut.

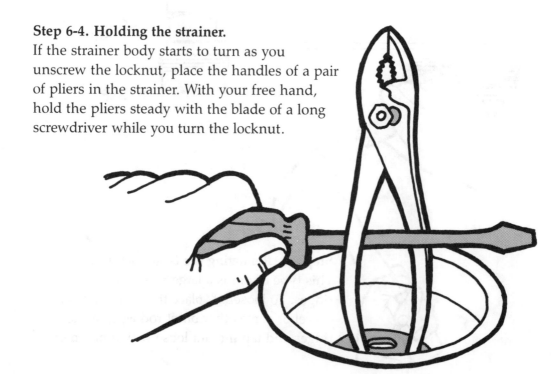

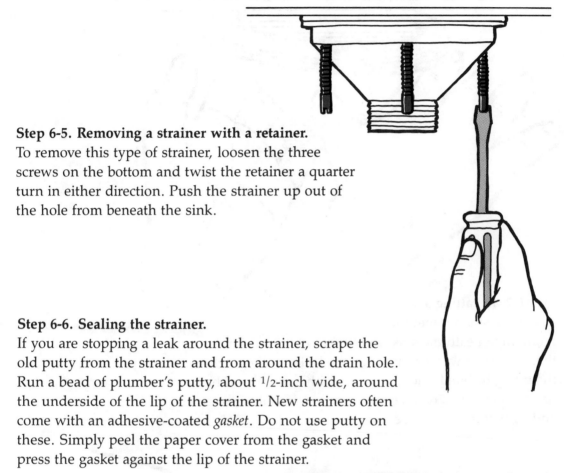

Step 6-5. Removing a strainer with a retainer.
To remove this type of strainer, loosen the three
screws on the bottom and twist the retainer a quarter
turn in either direction. Push the strainer up out of
the hole from beneath the sink.

Step 6-6. Sealing the strainer.
If you are stopping a leak around the strainer, scrape the
old putty from the strainer and from around the drain hole.
Run a bead of plumber's putty, about 1/2-inch wide, around
the underside of the lip of the strainer. New strainers often
come with an adhesive-coated *gasket*. Do not use putty on
these. Simply peel the paper cover from the gasket and
press the gasket against the lip of the strainer.

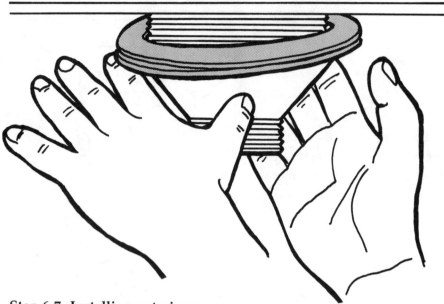

Step 6-7. Installing a strainer.

Lower the strainer into the hole in the sink.
From underneath the sink, install the rubber washer,
then the metal washer, and then the locknut. First tighten
the fitting by hand; then tighten it with a dowel and hammer
or a wrench. On a retainer-type strainer, install the retainer
and tighten the three screws.

Step 6-8. Completing the job.

Lift the tailpiece into position and tighten the coupling
nuts. Carefully remove any excess putty with a
putty knife and wipe the rim clean with a rag.

Step 6-9. Removing a slotted stopper.
To remove this type of pop-up stopper,
raise the stopper to its full open position,
twist the stopper counterclockwise, and
lift it out. Don't force it. It might not be
slotted. You might have to remove the
pivot rod beneath the sink.

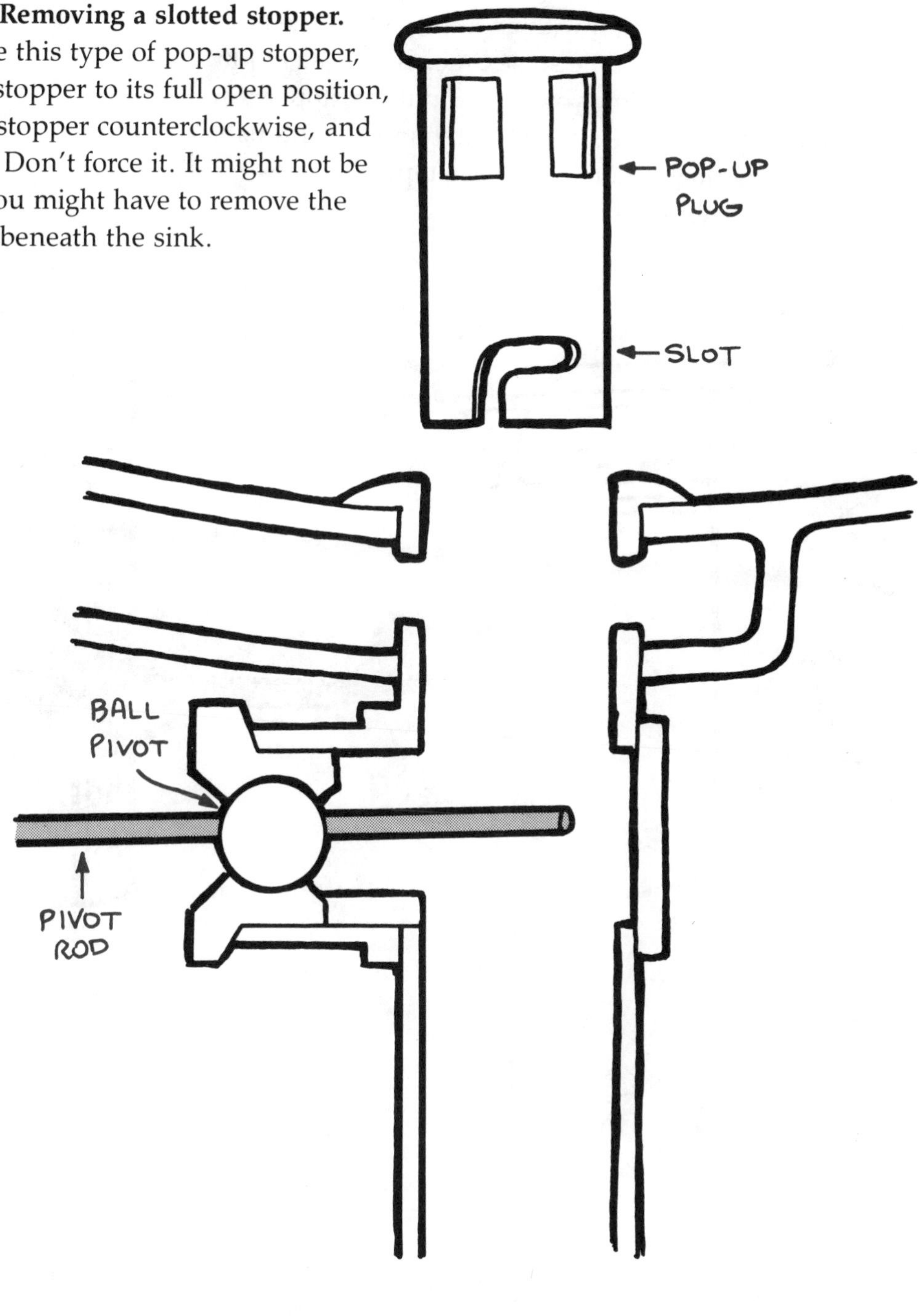

← POP-UP
PLUG

←SLOT

BALL
PIVOT

PIVOT
ROD

Step 6-10. Removing a pivot rod.

With the drain partially open, unscrew the nut
from the back of the drain with an adjustable wrench.
Squeeze the clip and, at the same time, slide the *pivot rod*
back from the drain. Now you can lift out the stopper.
Clean the stopper with soap and water and a stiff brush.
Replace any O-rings and reinstall the stopper.
Twist a slotted stopper into position.

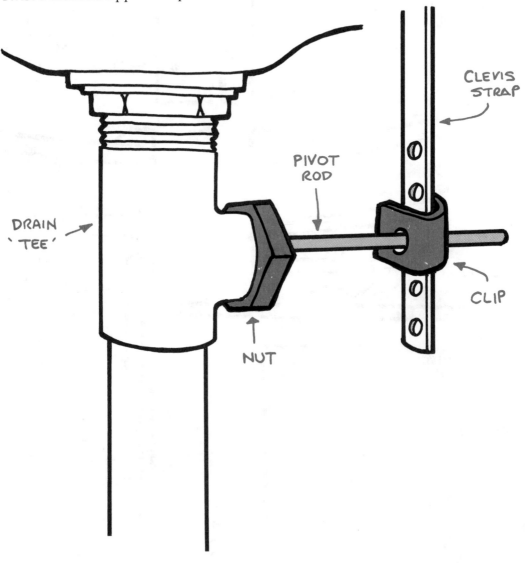

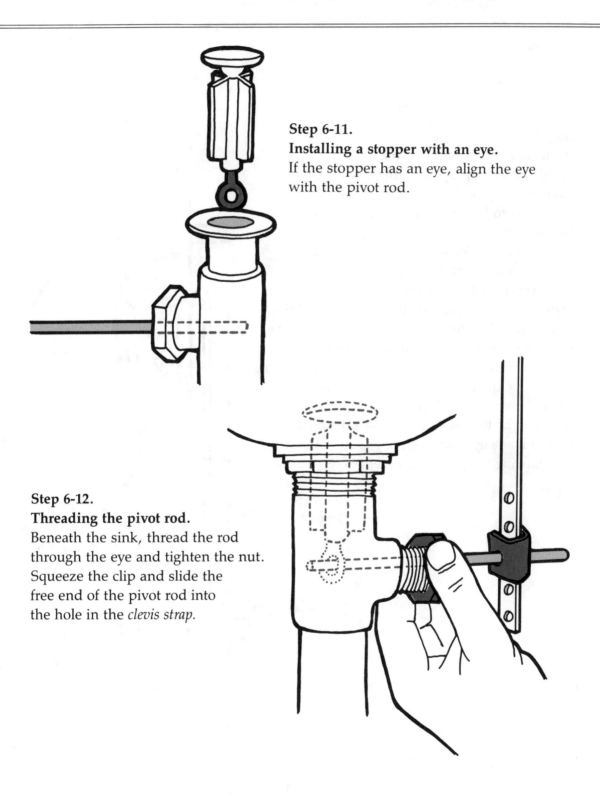

Step 6-11.
Installing a stopper with an eye.
If the stopper has an eye, align the eye with the pivot rod.

Step 6-12.
Threading the pivot rod.
Beneath the sink, thread the rod through the eye and tighten the nut. Squeeze the clip and slide the free end of the pivot rod into the hole in the *clevis strap*.

Step 6-13.

Adjusting the pop-up assembly.

To adjust the pop-up assembly, locate the
clevis screw up behind the back of the sink.
Use pliers to loosen the screw, then turn it
by hand. If the stopper fails to make a good
seal, move the clevis strap up the lift rod
to shorten the linkage. If the stopper doesn't
open far enough, move the strap down to permit
faster drainage. After you have determined the
proper length of the connection, tighten the clevis
screw and check the operation of the stopper.
If it is hard to open and close, squeeze the spring
clip to free the pivot rod from the clevis strap.
Slide the strap out a little way from the drain to
increase the leverage. Additional adjustments
can be made by removing the rod from the strap
and moving the rod to a different hole.

LIFT
ROD

CLEVIS
SCREW

CLEVIS
STRAP

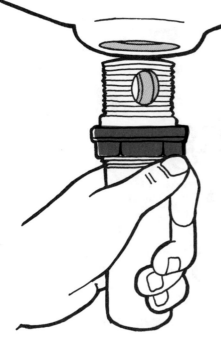

Step 6-14. Removing a drain.

To remove a drain, first place a bucket under the trap to catch water; then remove the trap and pop-up assembly. Loosen the locknut holding the drain to the sink. Push the drain up a little and remove the sink flange. Lower the drain from the opening in the sink.

Step 6-15. Replacing a drain.

Scrape the old putty from the drain opening and wipe the excess away with a rag. Install the new flange with the gasket that came with it, or run a bead of putty on the underside of the flange. Reconnect the drain assembly in the reverse order.

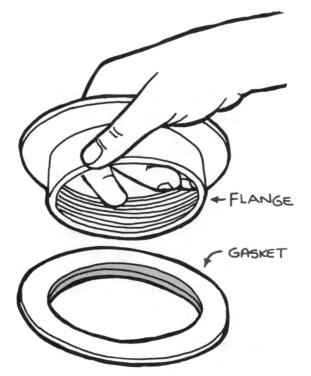

←FLANGE

ᴦGASKET

CHAPTER SEVEN

Unjamming Garbage Disposals

Garbage disposals often receive heavy use, but they will last many years if not abused. Basically, a garbage disposal consists of a motor turning a perforated metal disc, sometimes called a turntable or grinding wheel, equipped with impeller blades. When the garbage is dropped down the sink, it falls on the spinning turntable. It is then thrown outward to be caught between the impeller blades and the cutting edges of the grinding ring. There the garbage is shredded into pieces small enough to be washed down through the holes in the turntable and out the drain.

Before attempting any repair, make sure that the power is off at the service panel or that the unit is unplugged beneath the sink.

Tools & Materials

☐ Broom or plunger
☐ Ice cubes

Step 7-1. Freeing a jammed disposal.

To free a jammed disposal, turn off the switch and place the handle of a broom or plunger in the disposal. Push the end against an impeller blade and try to rotate the turntable in a counterclockwise direction. Don't push down too hard—you could dislodge the disposal from the sink.

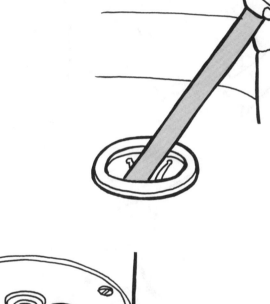

Step 7-2. Resetting the disposal.

Once the turntable moves freely, press the reset button on the bottom of the disposal. Run cold water down the drain and turn on the disposal.

Step 7-3. Using ice cubes.

If greasy foods have caused the jam, drop several ice cubes
down the drain and run the disposal. The ice will congeal the fat
and the disposal will grind it into small pieces.

To keep your unit running efficiently and safely:

- Don't use chemical drain cleaners in disposals—the cleaners can
  damage rubber and plastic parts.
- Keep the unit clean and fresh-smelling by grinding up citrus rind
  and by not allowing garbage to stay in the disposal overnight.
- Run cold water while the unit is operating.
- Use a drain cover to prevent kitchen utensils and other objects
  from falling in.
- Never attempt to retrieve a dropped utensil while the unit is running.

CHAPTER EIGHT

Replacing Garbage Disposals

G arbage disposals will last for many years with proper care, but they are easy to replace when the time comes. The only problem you might have is the cramped working conditions under the sink. Before starting to work, make sure that the power is off. Spread a few old newspapers under the disposal and have a bucket or pan handy to catch any excess water.

Tools & Materials
- ☐ Bucket or pan
- ☐ Screwdriver
- ☐ Pliers
- ☐ Pipe wrench
- ☐ Adjustable wrench
- ☐ New disposal

Step 8-1.
Disconnecting the dishwasher hose.
Disconnect the dishwasher drain hose from the disposal. Use a screwdriver or pliers, depending on the type of clamp.

CLAMP

DISHWASHER HOSE

DRAIN PIPE

Step 8-2.
Disconnecting the drainpipe.
Use a screwdriver to remove the drain gasket flange and disconnect the drainpipe, or use a wrench to loosen the coupling nuts and remove the sink trap.

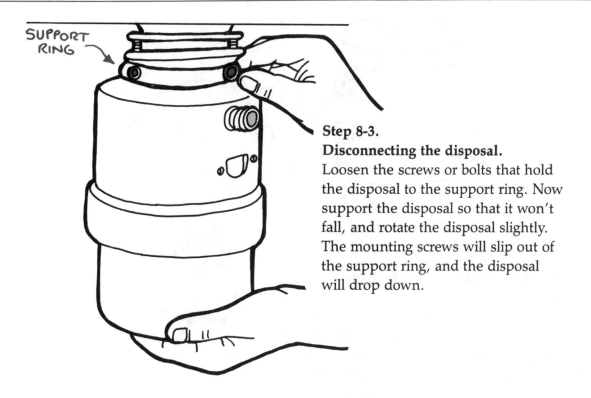

SUPPORT RING

Step 8-3.
Disconnecting the disposal.
Loosen the screws or bolts that hold
the disposal to the support ring. Now
support the disposal so that it won't
fall, and rotate the disposal slightly.
The mounting screws will slip out of
the support ring, and the disposal
will drop down.

Step 8-4.
Disconnecting the electrical connections.
Remove the cover plate on the bottom of disposal,
exposing the electrical connections. Disconnect
the wires. The wires must be reconnected
according to color. The green ground wire
connects to a screw mounted in the frame,
the white wire to the white wire, and the
black wire to the black wire. Use wire
nuts to make the new connections.

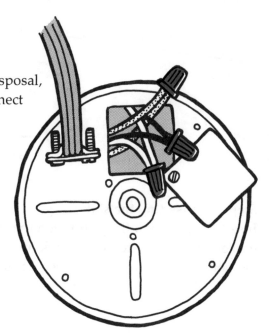

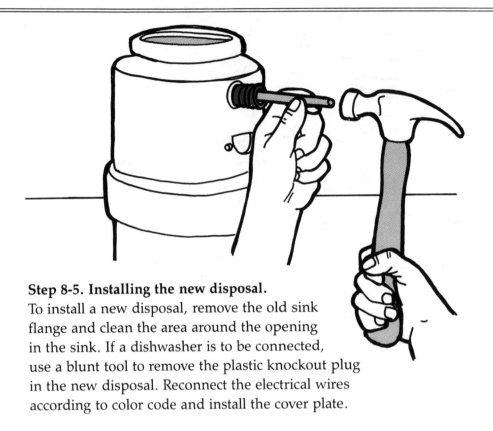

Step 8-5. Installing the new disposal.
To install a new disposal, remove the old sink flange and clean the area around the opening in the sink. If a dishwasher is to be connected, use a blunt tool to remove the plastic knockout plug in the new disposal. Reconnect the electrical wires according to color code and install the cover plate.

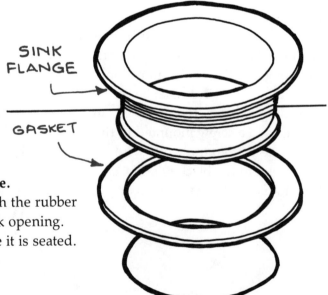

SINK
FLANGE

GASKET

Step 8-6. Inserting the sink flange.
Insert the new sink flange through the rubber gasket and into the top of the sink opening. Do not rotate the sink flange once it is seated.

Step 8-7. Attaching the support ring.

From beneath the sink, place the fiber gasket around the sink flange and screw the support ring into place.

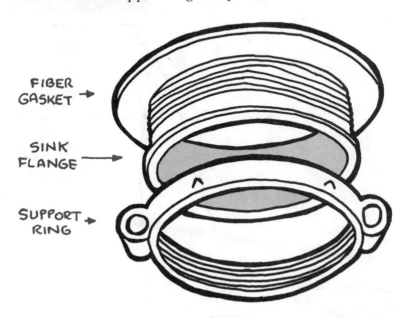

Step 8-8. Attaching the mounting ring.

Slide the mounting ring over the end of the sink flange.

Hold the ring up out of the way while you press the cushion mount over the lip on the sink flange. Now pull the mounting ring down over the cushion mount. The mounting ring should be free to rotate.

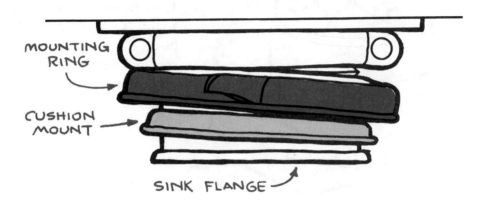

Step 8-9. Positioning the disposal.
Align the slots on the mounting ring with
the projections on the top of the disposal
and raise the disposal into position.

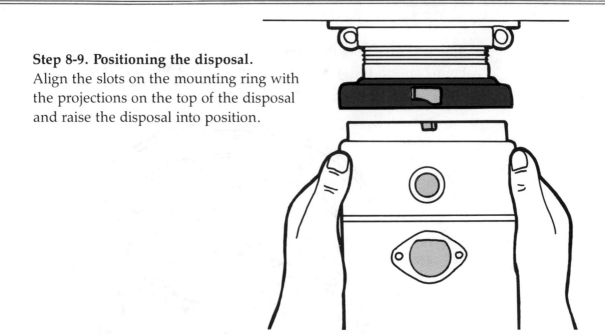

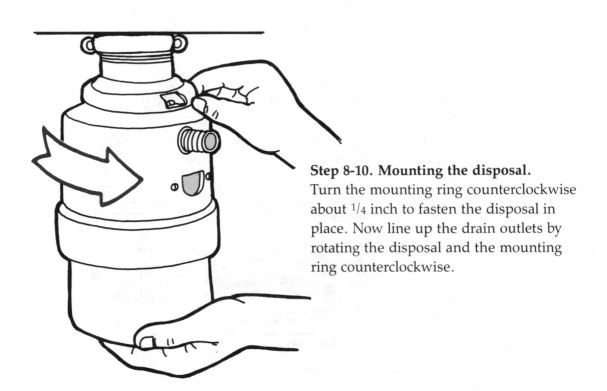

Step 8-10. Mounting the disposal.
Turn the mounting ring counterclockwise
about $1/4$ inch to fasten the disposal in
place. Now line up the drain outlets by
rotating the disposal and the mounting
ring counterclockwise.

Step 8-11. Locking the disposal.
Turn the mounting ring counterclockwise until the projections on the top of the disposal fit into the locked position in the slots in the mounting ring.

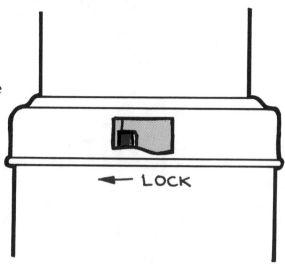

Step 8-12. Completing the job.
Connect the drainpipe to the disposal, or reinstall the trap. Reconnect the dishwasher hose and test the installation for leaks.

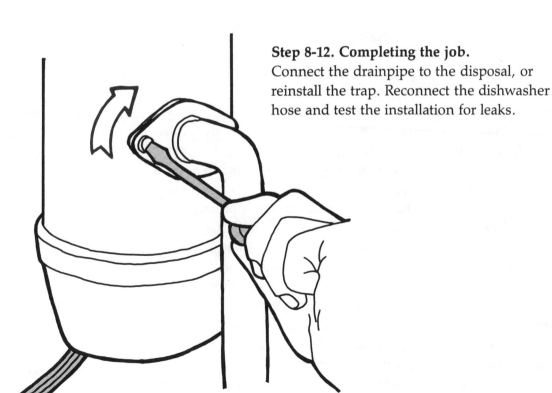

CHAPTER NINE

Repairing Tub & Shower Plumbing

R epairs to bathtub and shower plumbing often seem nearly impossible because the fittings are mysteriously hidden within the walls and the drains are inaccessible beneath the tub. But manufacturers have designed the plumbing to allow access when problems occur. Tub and shower faucets can be repaired from the front, and all tubs have an overflow tube that provides entry to a clogged drain. Problems usually consist of a leaky faucet or a dripping tub spout. Sometimes the shower diverter fails to send water to the shower head. Other problems might be a drain that is sluggish or clogged or a stopper that doesn't seal properly.

You can usually cure tub and shower plumbing problems with little more than a screwdriver, an adjustable wrench, and a pipe wrench. When making repairs, you'll probably have to stand in the tub. So before starting to work, close the drain to keep parts from disappearing down it, and spread a bath mat in the tub to protect the tub's finish.

Tools & Materials

- [ ] Two pipe wrenches
- [ ] Masking tape
- [ ] Screwdriver
- [ ] Vinegar
- [ ] Toothbrush
- [ ] Toothpick
- [ ] Adjustable wrench
- [ ] O-rings
- [ ] Hex wrench
- [ ] Spout
- [ ] Petroleum jelly
- [ ] Plunger
- [ ] Plumber's socket wrench
- [ ] Knife or small screwdriver
- [ ] Washers
- [ ] Replacement parts as needed

Step 9-1. Removing the shower head.

To clean a shower head, first remove it from the shower arm.
Use two wrenches and protect the chrome finish with tape.
Grip the shower arm with one wrench to hold it steady, and turn
the shower head collar counterclockwise with the other wrench.

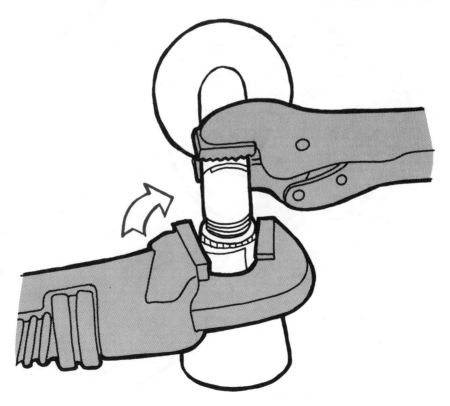

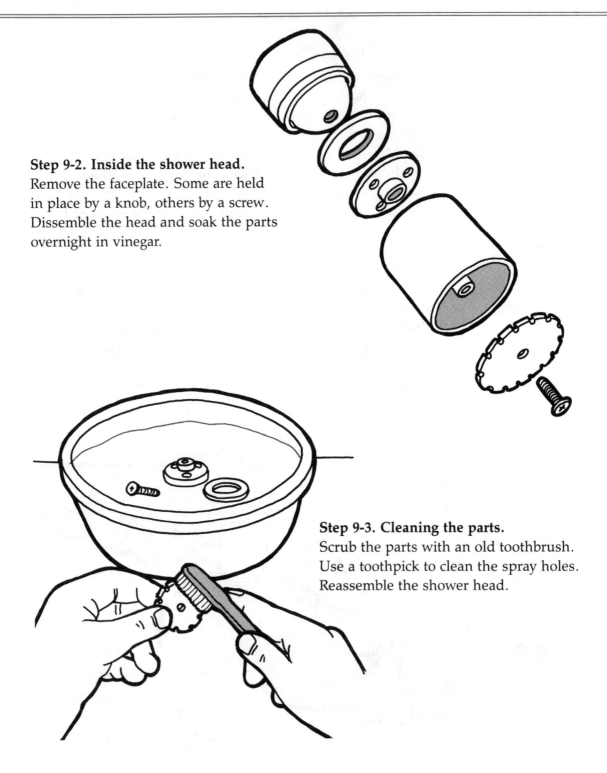

Step 9-2. Inside the shower head.
Remove the faceplate. Some are held
in place by a knob, others by a screw.
Dissemble the head and soak the parts
overnight in vinegar.

Step 9-3. Cleaning the parts.
Scrub the parts with an old toothbrush.
Use a toothpick to clean the spray holes.
Reassemble the shower head.

Step 9-4.

Removing and cleaning a stem diverter valve.
Diverter valves might be in the form of a valve stem or a simple *gate valve* in the tub spout. To repair a stem diverter valve, first turn off the water supply and open the faucets. If the tub does not have shutoff valves, turn off the main water supply valve to the house. Remove any handle or cover, and use an adjustable wrench to remove the stem. Clean any sediment from the parts with vinegar and an old toothbrush. Replace any O-rings and reinstall the valve.

O-RINGS

Step 9-5. Repairing a spout-gate diverter valve.
If the diverter valve is in the spout, replace the spout. First check for a setscrew under the spout. If there is one, loosen it with a hex wrench and twist off the spout. Install the new spout in the reverse order. If the old spout doesn't have a setscrew, grip the spout with a pipe wrench and turn it counterclockwise. Remove the old spout and thread the new one on the pipe by hand. Protect the new spout with tape, and tighten it with a pipe wrench.

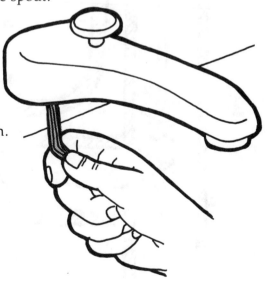

Bathtub drains come in two basic types: pop-up drains and trip-lever drains. The pop-up drain has a curved rocker arm inside the drain pipe connected to the stopper. The arm extends into a T where the end of the arm supports linkage connected to the control lever in the overflow plate. Raising and lowering the control lever allows the stopper to fall or rise to open and close the drain.

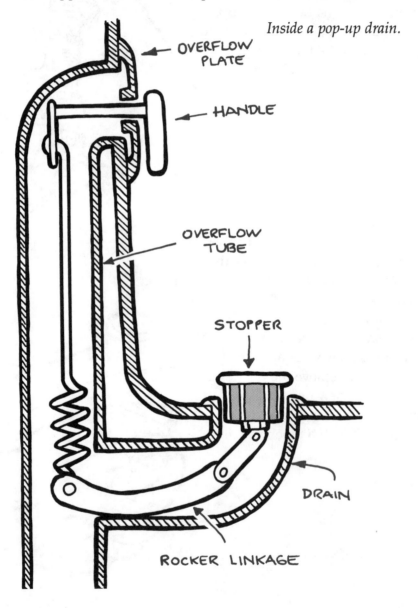

Inside a pop-up drain.

OVERFLOW PLATE

HANDLE

OVERFLOW TUBE

STOPPER

DRAIN

ROCKER LINKAGE

The trip-lever drain has a strainer over the drain and has linkage similar to the pop-up drain inside the overflow tube. The main difference is a hollow brass plunger positioned near the T. When the control lever is raised, the plunger moves into the T, blocking the flow from the drain. When the lever is lowered, the plunger moves out of the T, allowing water to flow. The plunger is hollow from top to bottom so water can always flow down the overflow tube.

Inside a trip-lever drain.

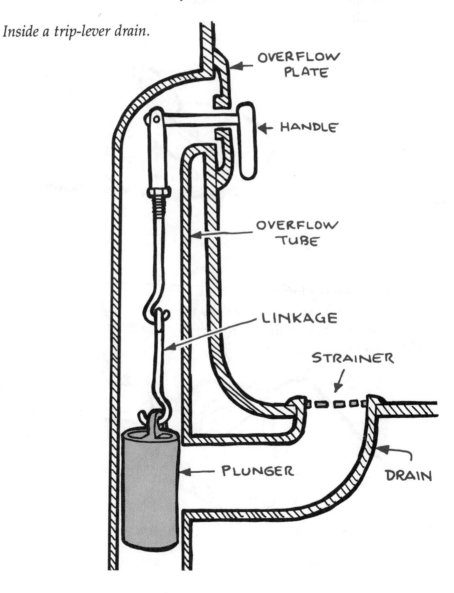

OVERFLOW PLATE

HANDLE

OVERFLOW TUBE

LINKAGE

STRAINER

PLUNGER

DRAIN

Step 9-6. Cleaning a pop-up stopper.

To clean a pop-up stopper, first move the control lever
to open the drain. Lift the stopper and slide the rocker arm
out the drain opening. Clean the stopper and drain opening
with fine steel wool and reinsert the stopper.
Keep the curve in the rocker arm down.
You might have to wiggle it in and out
a little until it slips into place.

Step 9-7. Removing the lift assembly.

To remove the lift assembly, unscrew the screws
from the plate covering the overflow tube,
and lift the linkage up and out of the tube.

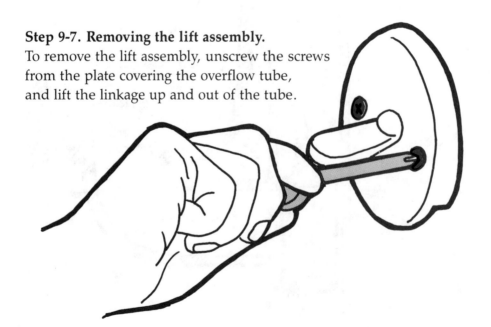

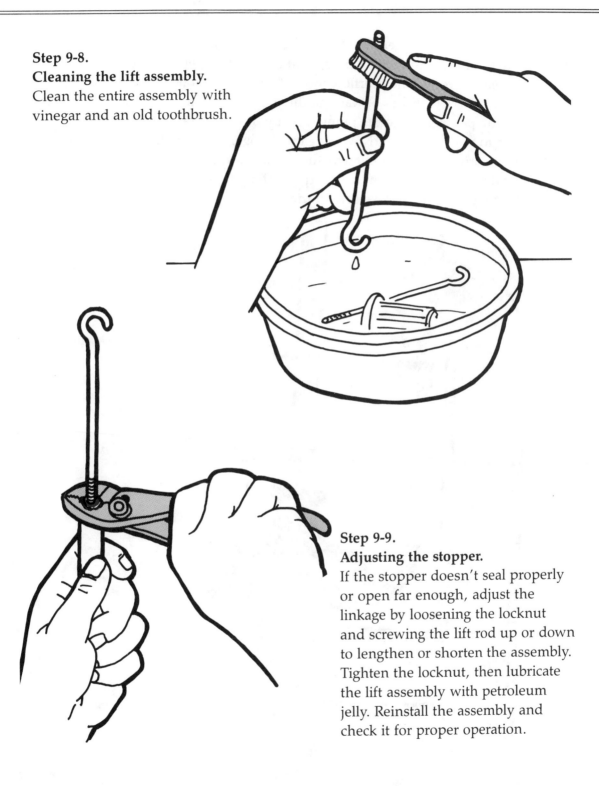

Step 9-8.
Cleaning the lift assembly.
Clean the entire assembly with vinegar and an old toothbrush.

Step 9-9.
Adjusting the stopper.
If the stopper doesn't seal properly or open far enough, adjust the linkage by loosening the locknut and screwing the lift rod up or down to lengthen or shorten the assembly. Tighten the locknut, then lubricate the lift assembly with petroleum jelly. Reinstall the assembly and check it for proper operation.

Step 9-10. Opening a clogged tub drain.

First, try to clear the drain with a plunger. If it has a stopper, remove it and the plate covering the overflow tube. Plug the overflow with a wet rag and run a few inches of water in the tub—enough to cover the cup of the plunger. Place the plunger partly over the drain and push down to remove any air. Now slide the plunger over the drain and pull up abruptly. Try not to break the plunger's seal over the drain. Continue pushing down and sharply pulling up until the clog is free. Be patient—it might take several tries.

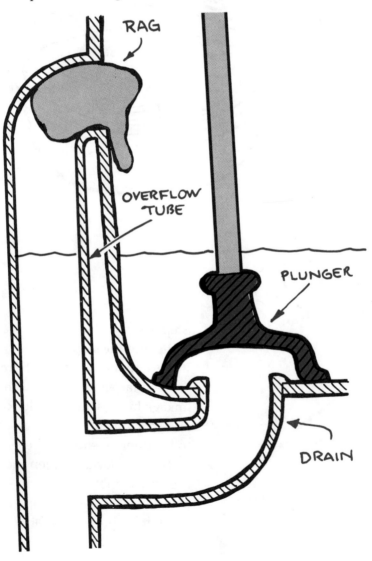

RAG

OVERFLOW TUBE

PLUNGER

DRAIN

Step 9-11. Clearing a tub drain with an auger.

If the plunger fails to unclog a tub drain, try to remove the blockage with an auger. Some of the debris might be snagged and pulled from the drain, so have a bucket or something handy to catch the debris when it comes out. Remove the stopper and lift assembly and run the auger into the overflow tube. Rotate the auger clockwise, carefully working it in and out to maneuver it through bends in the pipe. Once the clog is free, remove the auger and flush the drain with water.

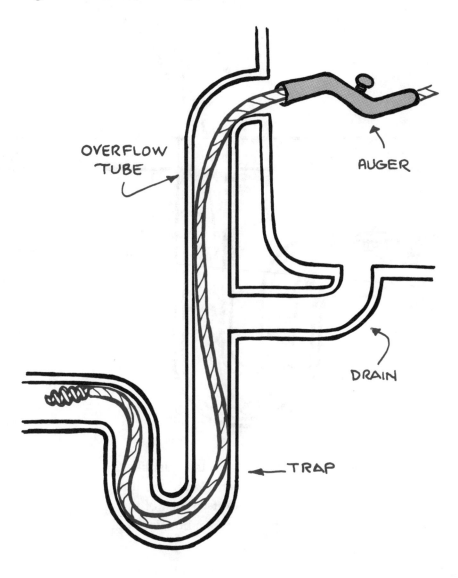

Step 9-12. Clearing a shower drain with an auger.
To clear a shower drain, which has no overflow tube,
remove the strainer and feed the auger into the drain.
Be sure to have a bucket handy for any debris
that might come out with the auger.

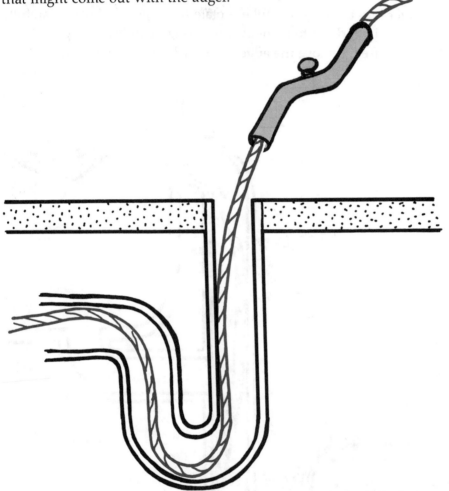

Repairing tub and shower faucets is just like fixing sink faucets.
The problem is getting to the stem. First, you'll need a deep socket
and ratchet—or a plumber's socket wrench of the appropriate size—
to remove the bonnet. The *bonnet* is a housing that contains most
of the stem.

Step 9-13. Getting to the bonnet.

First, turn off the water supply and open the faucet.
Then, pry off the handle cover with the tip of a knife or
small screwdriver. Now remove the screw, handle, and sleeve.
You should see the bonnet packing nut. It might be covered
with joint cement or plaster. If so, carefully chip the material
away to allow room for the socket wrench.

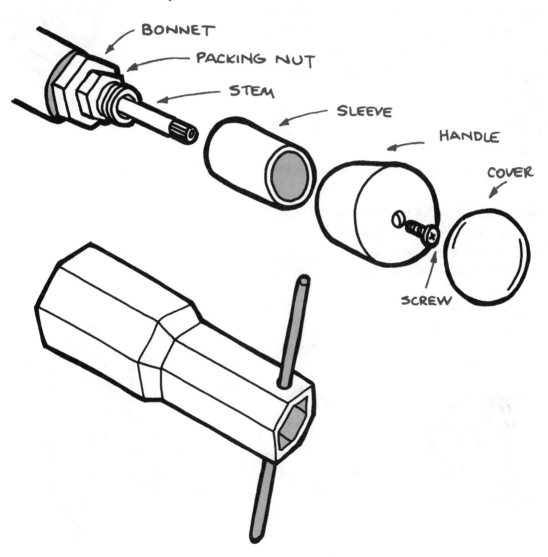

BONNET

PACKING NUT

STEM

SLEEVE

HANDLE

COVER

SCREW

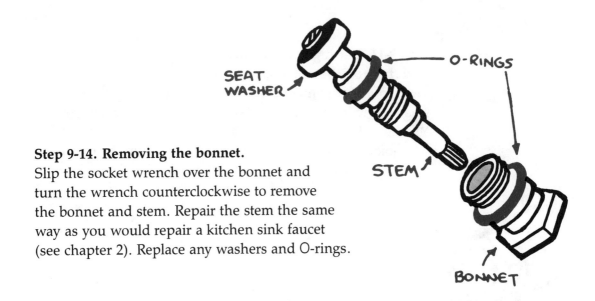

SEAT WASHER

O-RINGS

STEM

BONNET

Step 9-14. Removing the bonnet.
Slip the socket wrench over the bonnet and
turn the wrench counterclockwise to remove
the bonnet and stem. Repair the stem the same
way as you would repair a kitchen sink faucet
(see chapter 2). Replace any washers and O-rings.

Step 9-15. Dressing the faucet seat.
If necessary, dress or replace the faucet seat.
You can repair ball-type faucets and cartridge-type
faucets the same way you would fix kitchen sink faucets.

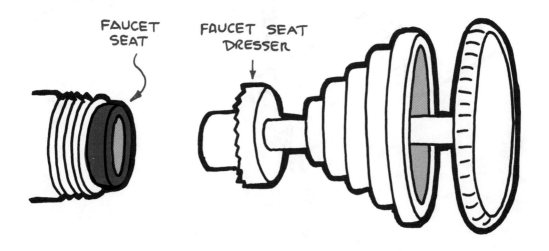

FAUCET SEAT

FAUCET SEAT DRESSER

CHAPTER TEN

Repairing Toilets

Toilets operate on a simple principle: They use a lever to trip a *flush valve*, which releases a volume of water from a tank. The water swirls into a bowl, then travels through a water-filled trap into a waste line. As the water leaves the tank, a float drops down and opens another valve, called a *ball cock*, causing a smaller flow of water to refill the tank. At the same time, gravity closes the flush valve. When the water reaches a certain level, the float closes the ball cock, shutting off the water to the tank, and the system is ready to use again.

The tank and bowl are made of porcelain and will last almost forever. However, the parts inside the tank that operate the system are made of brass or plastic, and they will eventually corrode or wear out and need replacing. The most common problems are the water running continuously after the toilet has been flushed and the toilet failing to flush completely. And occasionally, leaks from the tank do occur.

Tools & Materials

- [ ] Pliers
- [ ] Screwdriver
- [ ] Fine steel wool
- [ ] Knife
- [ ] Toothbrush
- [ ] Vinegar
- [ ] Washers and bolts
- [ ] Adjustable wrench
- [ ] Locking pliers
- [ ] Plumber's putty
- [ ] Food coloring
- [ ] Putty knife
- [ ] Rubber gloves
- [ ] Silicone sealant (optional)
- [ ] Gasket with plastic sleeve (optional)

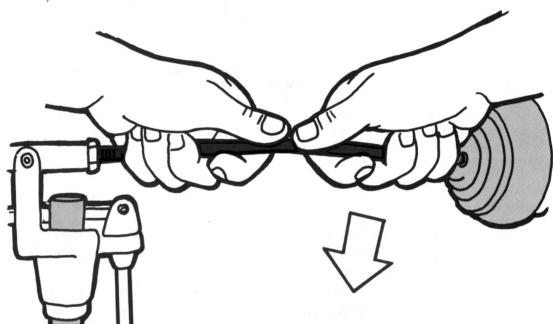

Step 10-1. Adjusting the float.
When water continues to run in the tank, it usually means that the float is set for too high a water level. To adjust the level, grasp the float arm and carefully bend it down—just a little—with your fingers. Now flush the toilet and check the new water level. It should be about 1/2 inch below the top of the overflow tube. If the level is too low, bend the arm up slightly. Plastic arms have an adjustment knob to raise or lower the float. Sometimes a float will develop a leak and take in water.

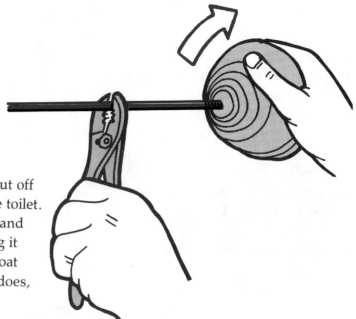

Step 10-2.
Checking the float for leaks.
To check the float for leaks, shut off the water supply and flush the toilet. Hold the float arm with pliers and remove the float by unscrewing it counterclockwise. Shake the float to see if it has water in it. If it does, replace it.

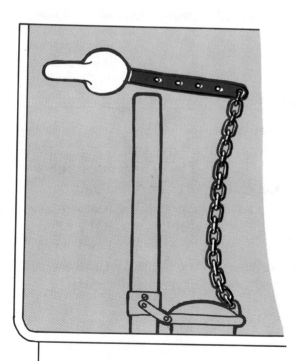

Step 10-3.
Adjusting the handle.
If the handle must be held down to flush the toilet, the linkage needs to be shortened. If the linkage is a chain, try connecting it to a different hole in the trip arm. Or use pliers to cut off a few links. On some models, you can adjust the linkage by loosening the clamping screw on a guide arm, then raising or lowering the guide arm. Retighten the screw after you've positioned the handle properly.

Step 10-4.
Stopping the flush valve from leaking.
When water runs continuously from the tank into the bowl, the flush valve is probably not sealing properly. It might be a *flapper* or *ball* valve. To clean the valve seat, first turn off the water supply and flush the toilet to empty the tank. Unhook the flapper—or loosen the clamp screw—and slide the valve up the overflow tube.

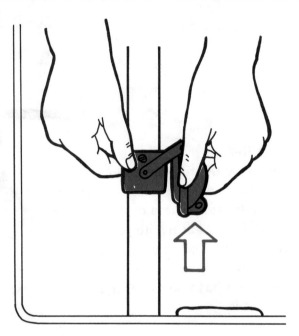

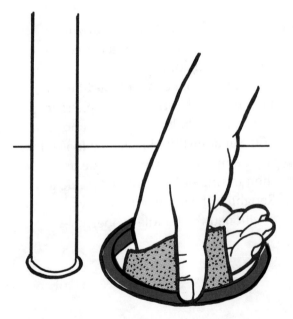

Step 10-5.
Cleaning the valve seat.
Use fine steel wool to gently scrub any mineral deposits or sediment from the valve seat. Wash the sediment into the bowl and reinstall the valve. Turn on the water supply and check for leaks. If the flapper, or ball, is badly worn or distorted, replace it.

Step 10-6. Removing a ball cock with a plunger.

To repair the ball cock, first shut off the water supply and flush the toilet. For a ball cock with a plunger, remove the two thumbscrews and slide out the float arm. Now lift out the plunger.

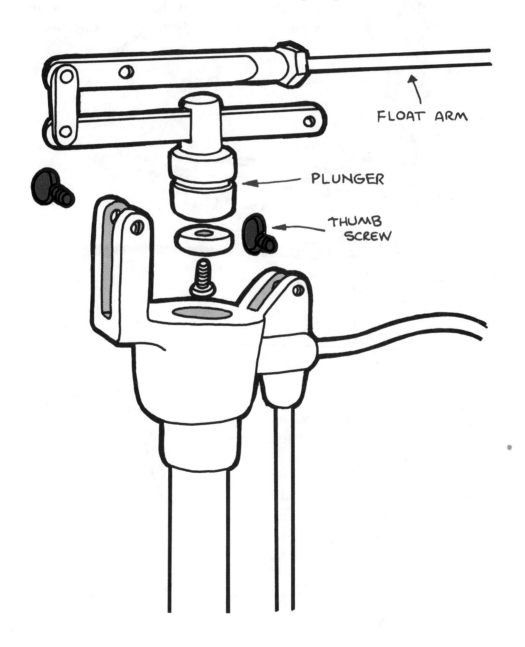

FLOAT ARM

PLUNGER

THUMB SCREW

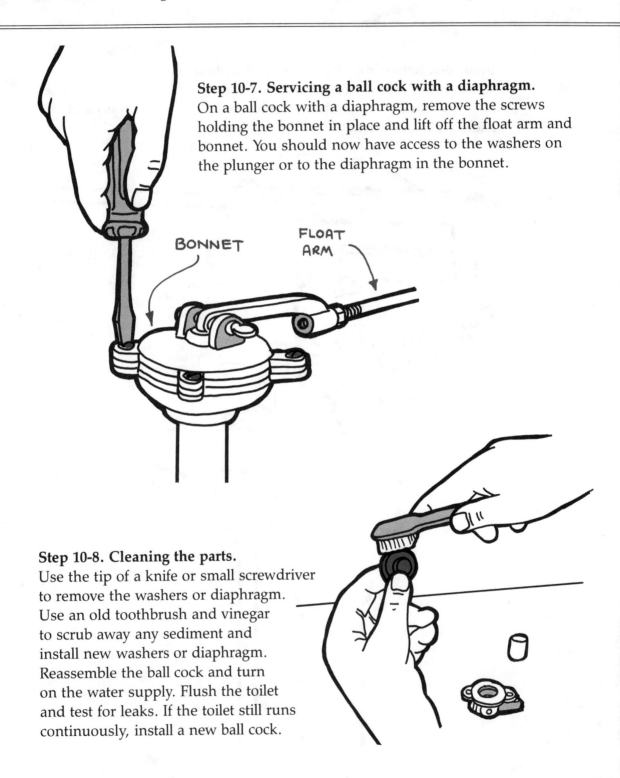

Step 10-7. Servicing a ball cock with a diaphragm.
On a ball cock with a diaphragm, remove the screws
holding the bonnet in place and lift off the float arm and
bonnet. You should now have access to the washers on
the plunger or to the diaphragm in the bonnet.

BONNET

FLOAT
ARM

Step 10-8. Cleaning the parts.
Use the tip of a knife or small screwdriver
to remove the washers or diaphragm.
Use an old toothbrush and vinegar
to scrub away any sediment and
install new washers or diaphragm.
Reassemble the ball cock and turn
on the water supply. Flush the toilet
and test for leaks. If the toilet still runs
continuously, install a new ball cock.

To replace the ball cock, first shut off the water and flush the toilet. Drain as much water from the tank as you can and sponge up any excess. Unscrew the float arm and float from the ball cock. Next you need to disconnect the water supply tube underneath the tank.

Step 10-9. Disconnecting the supply tube.
Use an adjustable wrench to disconnect the water supply tube from the tank. You might need to disconnect the tube from the shutoff valve and remove it completely.

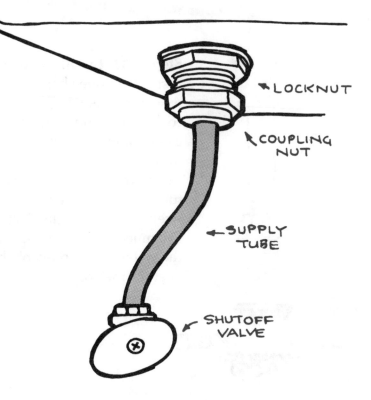

LOCKNUT

COUPLING NUT

SUPPLY TUBE

SHUTOFF VALVE

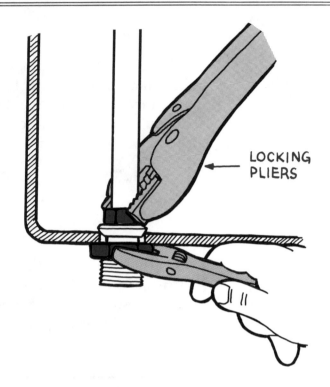

LOCKING PLIERS

Step 10-10.
Removing the old ball cock.
Inside the tank, grip the ball cock at its base with locking pliers. Use an adjustable wrench to unscrew the locknut under the tank. Now lift the ball cock from the tank.

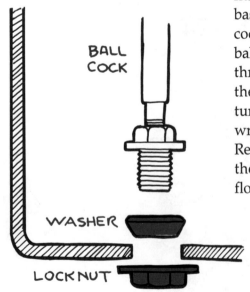

BALL COCK

WASHER

LOCKNUT

Step 10-11. Installing the new ball cock.
Install the cone-shaped washer on the threaded base of the new ball cock. Then insert the ball cock into the opening in the tank. Hold the ball cock in position with one hand while you thread the locknut on with the other. Tighten the locknut as tight as you can by hand, then turn it about a half turn with an adjustable wrench. Reinstall the float arm and float. Reconnect the water supply tube and turn on the water. You'll probably have to adjust the float for the correct water level.

Step 10-12. Stopping leaks from the tank.

A tank can leak in three or four places. The most common one is at the base of the ball cock. The other places include the tank mounting bolts and the flush valve. If you can't tell where the leak is coming from, drop a few drops of food coloring into the tank and let it stand overnight. To repair a leaking ball cock, try tightening the locknut under the tank about a quarter turn. Hold the ball cock with one hand and tighten the locknut with the other.

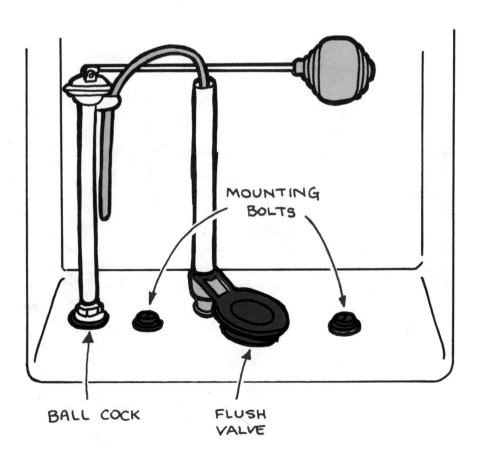

MOUNTING
BOLTS

BALL COCK   FLUSH
VALVE

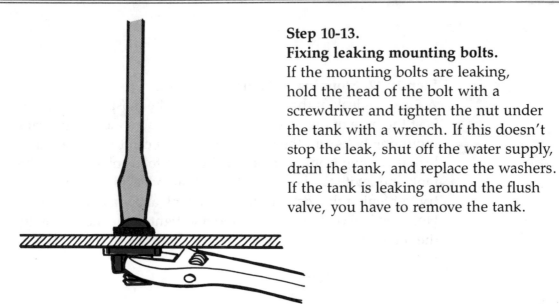

Step 10-13.
Fixing leaking mounting bolts.
If the mounting bolts are leaking,
hold the head of the bolt with a
screwdriver and tighten the nut under
the tank with a wrench. If this doesn't
stop the leak, shut off the water supply,
drain the tank, and replace the washers.
If the tank is leaking around the flush
valve, you have to remove the tank.

Step 10-14.
Disconnecting and removing the tank.
To disconnect the tank, shut off the water
supply, flush the toilet, and sponge any
excess water from the tank. Disconnect
the water supply tube from the tank.
Hold the head of the hold-down bolts
with a screwdriver and remove the nuts
beneath the tank with a wrench. Remove
the tank by lifting it straight up from the bowl.

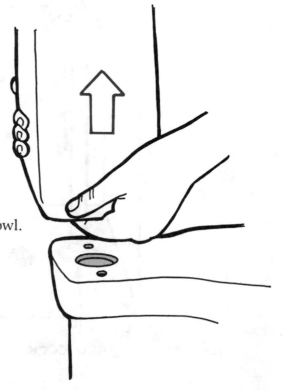

Step 10-15. Completing the job.

Remove the locknut on the bottom of the tank, and take out the flush valve from inside the tank. Scrape off the old washer and gasket material and install a new flush valve. Now carefully place the tank back on the bowl and install new washers and bolts. Reconnect the water supply tube and turn the water back on. Check for leaks.

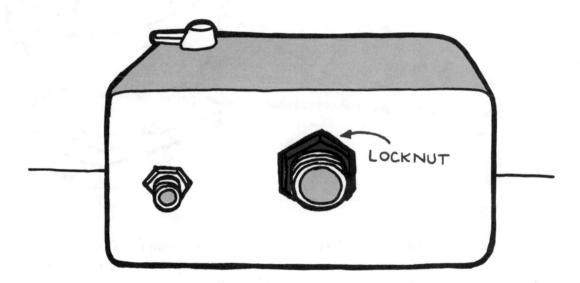

If water appears on the floor around the bowl, the wax gasket is probably leaking. To replace it, you have to remove the toilet, which is not a complicated operation, but might take two people a half day to complete. You'll probably work more comfortably wearing rubber gloves. Have a few old newspapers handy to keep the floor clean. First turn off the water supply and flush the toilet. Drain all the water from the tank.

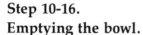

Step 10-16.
Emptying the bowl.
With the tank empty, use a plunger to push the water from the bowl. Try to remove as much water as possible.

Step 10-17. Disconnecting the bowl from the floor.
Disconnect and remove the water supply tube from the tank and shutoff valve. The two bolts holding the toilet to the floor are usually hidden beneath decorative caps. Lift or pry off the caps and use a wrench to remove the nuts.

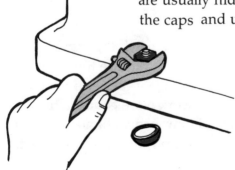

Step 10-18. Removing the toilet from the drain.
With a person on each side of the bowl, gently rock the toilet to
break the seal. Then lift the toilet straight up four or five inches,
and carefully lay it to one side. You might cover the open drain
to prevent fumes from escaping.

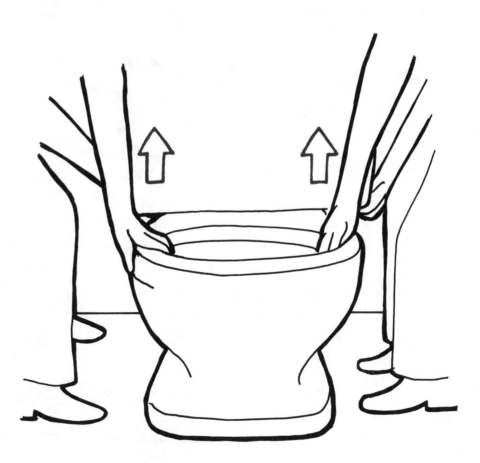

Step 10-19.
Removing the old seal.
Use a putty knife to remove the old wax seal from the bottom of the bowl and the flange in the floor. At this time, you can run a bead of plumber's putty around the bottom edge of the rim of the toilet. Or you can seal the crack between the toilet and the floor with silicone sealant after the toilet has been installed.

OLD
WAX SEAL

Step 10-20.
Installing a new seal.
Turn the new wax seal so that the tapered side is up and press it over the drain opening in the bottom of the bowl. If you have a 4-inch drain in the floor, you might want to install a gasket that has a plastic sleeve. The sleeve fits down into the drain and seals any cracks in the pipe.

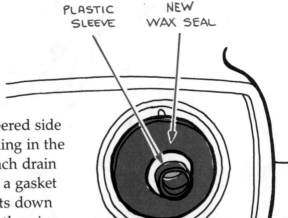

PLASTIC
SLEEVE

NEW
WAX SEAL

Step 10-21. Aligning the bolts.
Make sure the bolts are lined up
in the floor flange.

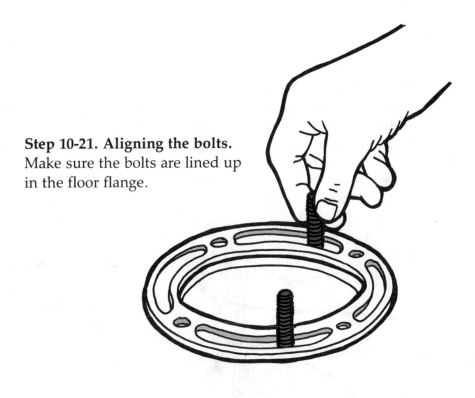

Step 10-22. Completing the job.
Carefully lower the toilet straight down onto
the floor flange. Have someone sit on the seat
and slowly rock back and forth in all
directions to spread the wax seal evenly.
Install the washers and nuts on the bolts,
and tighten them by hand. Use a wrench
to tighten them an additional quarter turn.

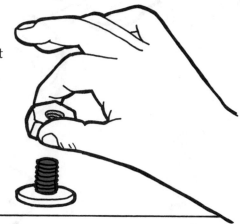

Step 10-23. Checking for leaks.
Wipe away any excess putty. Check the seal by pouring water into
the bowl. If it leaks, you have to install another new wax seal. If it
doesn't leak, reconnect the water supply tube and turn on the water.

CHAPTER ELEVEN

Working with Copper Tubing

C opper tubing is used in most homes to deliver water to the fixtures. It is lightweight, durable, and easy to work with. Long runs are normally soldered together, but compression fittings are often used when installing valves. Rigid copper tubing comes in 10-foot lengths, while flexible copper tubing is sold in rolls. Both are available, including fittings, in almost any size you need.

When working with copper tubing, you might need to use a propane torch. If you do use a propane torch, please take the following precautions:

1. Remember that propane fuel is extremely flammable.
2. Always follow the operating instructions that come with the torch.
3. Use the torch only in a well-ventilated area.
4. Protect any flammable surrounding materials with a fireproof shield.
5. Disconnect the cylinder from the valve when the torch is not in use.
6. Do not store the propane tank near heat or in an inhabited room.

Tools & Materials

- ☐ Copper tubing
- ☐ Tube bender
- ☐ Tube cutter
- ☐ Compression nut
- ☐ Compression ring
- ☐ Adjustable wrench
- ☐ Flaring tool
- ☐ Wire brush (optional)
- ☐ Emery cloth
- ☐ Flux
- ☐ Small brush
- ☐ Safety gloves
- ☐ Safety goggles
- ☐ Propane torch
- ☐ Solder

Step 11-1. Bending copper tubing.

To keep tubing from kinking when you bend it, slide a tube bender over the desired area of the bend. Slip the bender on the tube using a clockwise, twisting motion. Bend the tube with your thumbs and fingers or place it over your knee and bend it with your hands.

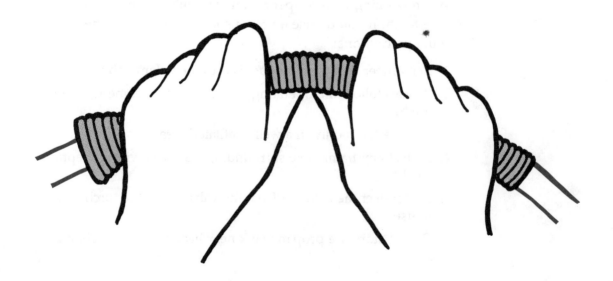

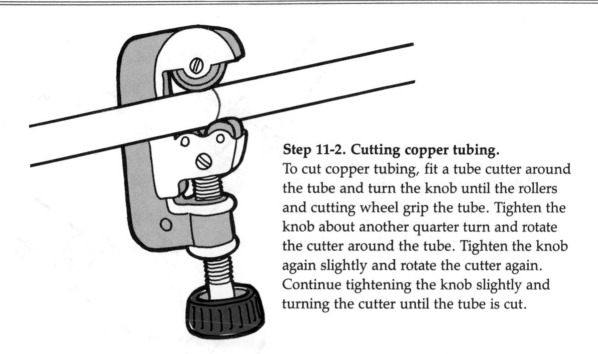

Step 11-2. Cutting copper tubing.
To cut copper tubing, fit a tube cutter around the tube and turn the knob until the rollers and cutting wheel grip the tube. Tighten the knob about another quarter turn and rotate the cutter around the tube. Tighten the knob again slightly and rotate the cutter again. Continue tightening the knob slightly and turning the cutter until the tube is cut.

Step 11-3. Using the reamer.
Inside the cut end of the copper tubing, you will notice a jagged burr. To remove the burr, you will need the triangular blade (reamer) on the side of the tube cutter. Swing out the blade and insert it into the tube. Twist the tube cutter, applying a little pressure, and ream out the burrs.

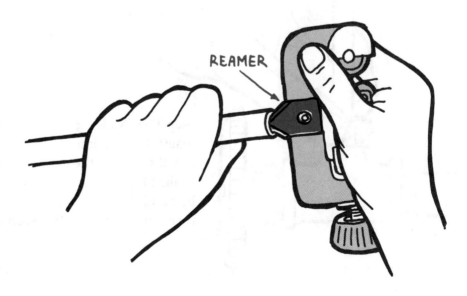

REAMER

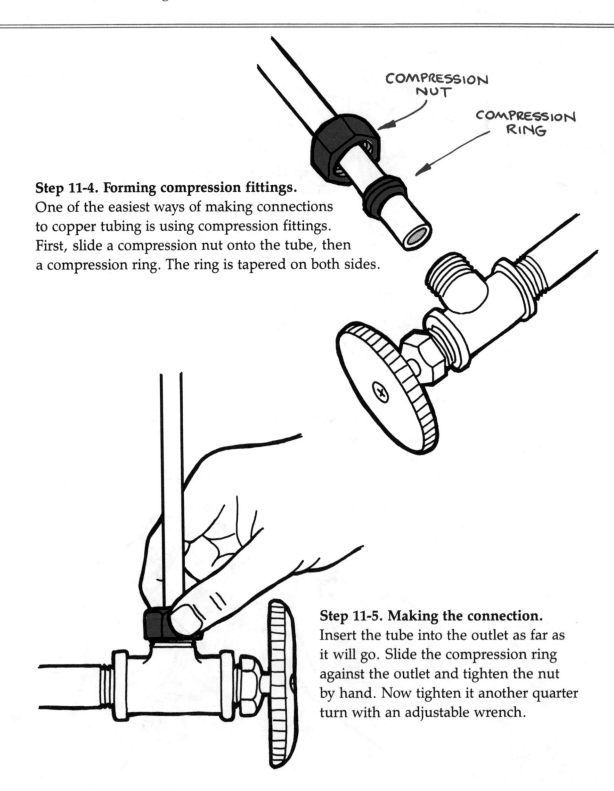

COMPRESSION
NUT

COMPRESSION
RING

Step 11-4. Forming compression fittings.
One of the easiest ways of making connections
to copper tubing is using compression fittings.
First, slide a compression nut onto the tube, then
a compression ring. The ring is tapered on both sides.

Step 11-5. Making the connection.
Insert the tube into the outlet as far as
it will go. Slide the compression ring
against the outlet and tighten the nut
by hand. Now tighten it another quarter
turn with an adjustable wrench.

Step 11-6. Forming flared fittings.

Another way to make connections in tubing is with a flared fitting. To flare the end of a tube, you need a flaring tool. First slide the compression nut onto the tube. Loosen the wing nuts on the flaring tool and open the die block. Place the tube into the proper opening (die) so that the end of the tube is just past the edge of the die. Tighten the wing nuts on the die block. Place the flaring tool so that the tapered head is inside the end of the tube. Now turn the handle clockwise and force the head into the tube to flare the end of the tube to about a 45-degree angle. Turn the handle counterclockwise, loosen the wing nuts and remove the tube. The compression nut and flared tube will now fit the tapered end of a flare connection.

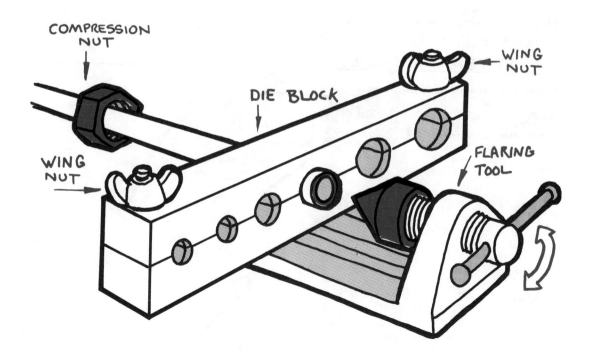

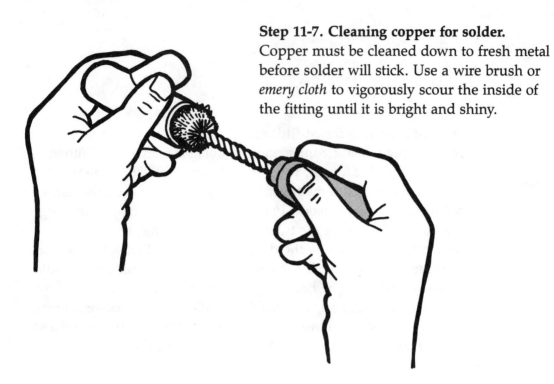

Step 11-7. Cleaning copper for solder.
Copper must be cleaned down to fresh metal
before solder will stick. Use a wire brush or
emery cloth to vigorously scour the inside of
the fitting until it is bright and shiny.

Step 11-8. Using emery cloth.
Use emery cloth to clean the end of the tube.
Wipe off any grit with a clean, dry rag.

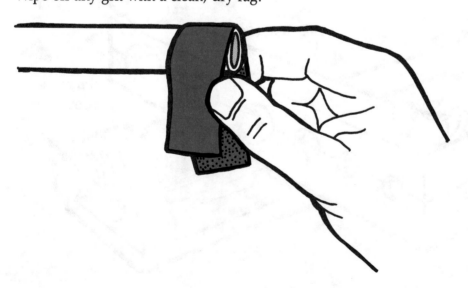

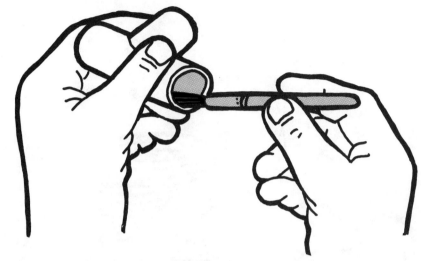

Step 11-9. Applying flux for soldering.

Use paste flux and a small brush to apply a thin film of flux to the inside of the fitting and the outside of the tube. Insert the end of the tube into the fitting as far as it will go. Now give the tube about a half twist to spread the flux evenly.

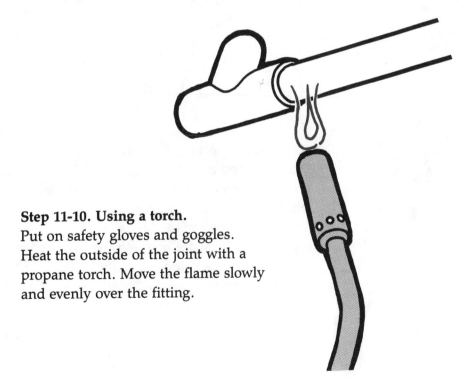

Step 11-10. Using a torch.

Put on safety gloves and goggles. Heat the outside of the joint with a propane torch. Move the flame slowly and evenly over the fitting.

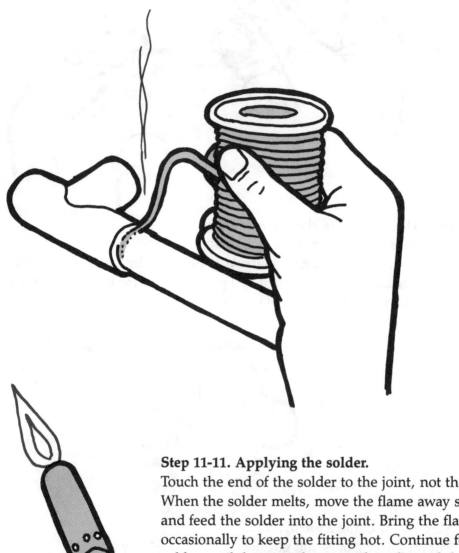

Step 11-11. Applying the solder.
Touch the end of the solder to the joint, not the flame.
When the solder melts, move the flame away slightly
and feed the solder into the joint. Bring the flame back
occasionally to keep the fitting hot. Continue feeding
solder until the space between the tube and the fitting
is completely filled and the solder begins to drip from
the joint. Wipe off the blackened flux with a wet rag.

CHAPTER TWELVE

Working with Plastic Pipe

Plastic pipes are generally known by the initials of their chemical makeup. For example, polyvinyl chloride goes by PVC and chlorinated polyvinyl chloride by CPVC. PVC pipe can be used in drain and vent systems and in cold water supply lines. CPVC pipe can be used for both hot and cold water supply lines. It is important not to mix the two together and to use the correct cement to make connections: PVC solvent cement for PVC pipe and CPVC solvent cement for CPVC pipe.

Tools & Materials
- ☐ Rigid plastic pipe, PVC or CPVC
- ☐ Fine-toothed hacksaw
- ☐ Fine sandpaper
- ☐ Small brush
- ☐ PVC solvent cement or CPVC solvent cement
- ☐ Teflon pipe tape
- ☐ Adapter

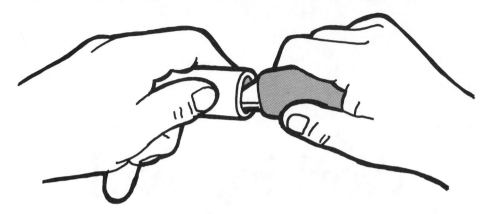

Step 12-1. Preparing the connection.
Cut rigid plastic pipe with a fine-toothed hacksaw. Use a knife to trim the inside of the cut end and to bevel the outside edge. Try out the fitting. The pipe should slide in easily but be snug enough not to fall out.

Step 12-2. Applying the solvent cement.
Use fine sandpaper to remove the surface gloss from the inside of the fitting and the outside of the pipe. Both parts should be clean and dry. Be sure you use the right cement for the pipe. Work quickly—this cement sets in about 10 seconds. With a small brush, apply a generous layer of cement to the outside of the pipe and a thin layer to the inside of the fitting.

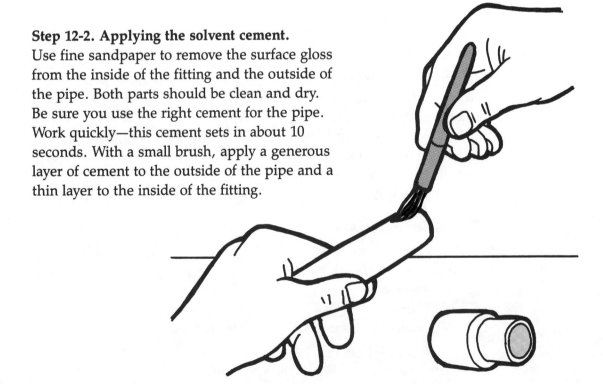

Step 12-3. Installing the fitting.

Insert the pipe into the fitting as far as it will go, and give the pipe about a quarter turn to spread the cement evenly. A bead of cement should form completely around the joint. If not, quickly remove the pipe and add more cement. Press the pieces together for about 10 seconds, then wipe off any excess cement with a rag. Let the connection cure for an hour or so before using.

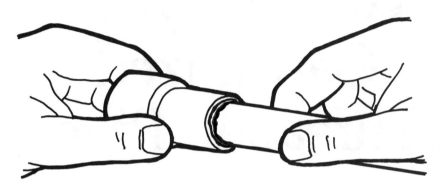

Step 12-4. Connecting plastic pipe to a threaded pipe.

Wrap about one and a half turns of pipe tape clockwise around the threads of the metal pipe. Screw the threaded end of an adapter onto the metal pipe by hand. Use an adjustable wrench to make the connection snug. Apply a layer of cement on the inside of the plastic-lined end of the adapter and on the outside of the end of the plastic pipe. Press the end of the pipe into the adapter as far as it will go and give the pipe about a quarter turn to spread the cement. Hold the pieces together for about 10 seconds.

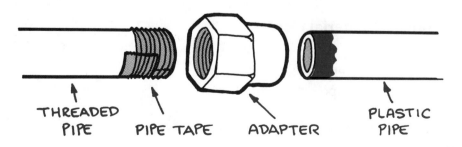

THREADED PIPE   PIPE TAPE   ADAPTER   PLASTIC PIPE

CHAPTER THIRTEEN

Working with Galvanized Threaded Pipe

Threaded pipe used in water lines is usually made of galvanized steel. It is easy to assemble. Just wrap the threads with pipe tape and tighten the connections with a couple of pipe wrenches. The problem comes when you have to remove a length of pipe. Because both ends of the pipe are threaded in the same direction, unscrewing one end only tightens the other end. So when a pipe develops a leak, you have to cut the damaged pipe and replace it with two new pipes and a union.

Tools & Materials
- ☐ Hacksaw
- ☐ Two pipe wrenches
- ☐ Galvanized pipe
- ☐ Union
- ☐ Teflon pipe tape

Step 13-1. Removing the damaged pipe.
Cut the pipe with a hacksaw. Hold the fitting steady with a pipe wrench and unscrew the cut pipe with another pipe wrench. Remove the other half of the cut pipe the same way. Take both pieces of the old pipe with you when you buy the replacement.

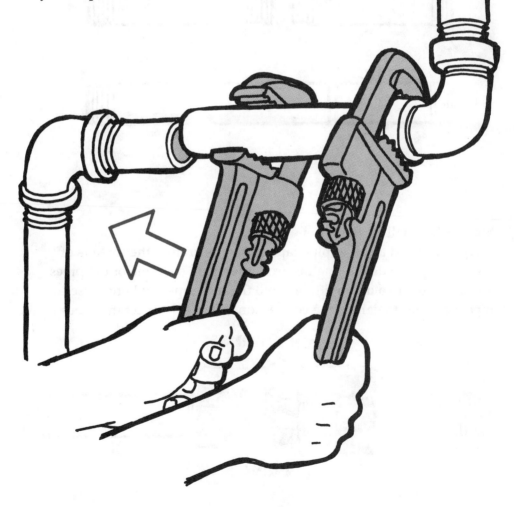

Step 13-2. Getting a replacement.

Match the size and length of the replacement to those of the old pipe.
You should have two new threaded pipes—which together equal the
length of the old pipe—and a union.

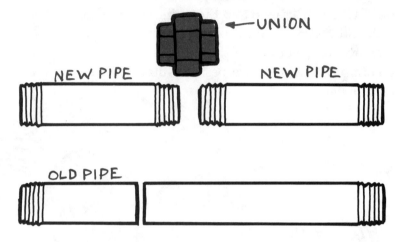

Step 13-3. Installing the union.

Wrap a turn and a half of pipe tape clockwise around the threads of
the new pipe. Slide the ring nut from the union over one of the pipes
and screw the two union fittings onto the new pipes by hand. Use two
pipe wrenches to tighten the connections. Do not connect the pipes.

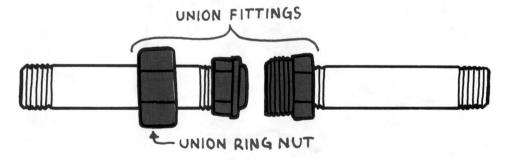

Step 13-4. Installing the replacement.
Screw the remaining ends of the new pipe into the fittings on the existing pipes and tighten the connections with two pipe wrenches. Now screw the ring nut onto the remaining threads of the union by hand and use two wrenches to tighten the connection.

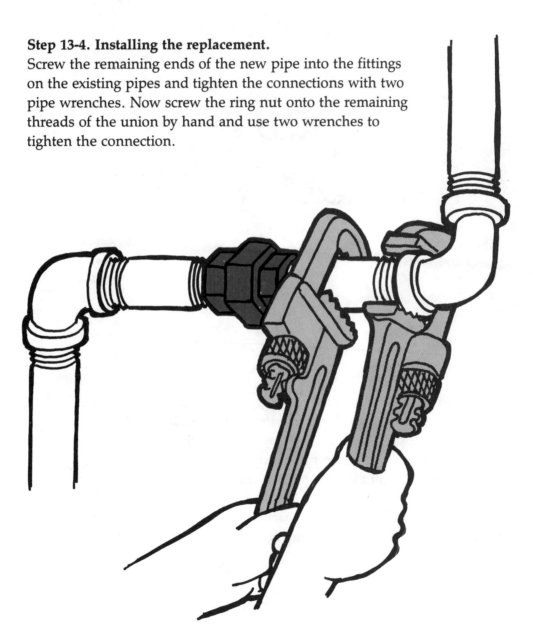

CHAPTER FOURTEEN

Repairing Shutoff Valves

S hutoff valves of two basic types are used in the home: a gate
valve and a globe valve. The *gate valve* is installed in the main
water supply line and is used as the main shutoff valve. When
this valve is open, it offers no resistance to the flow of water. It
should be operated in the full open or closed position. Otherwise,
the disc that acts as the gate can vibrate and chatter. The *globe valve*
will operate smoothly even when partially open. Globe valves are
installed in branch lines near fixtures.

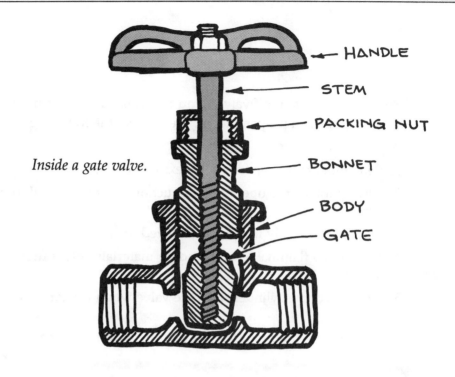

HANDLE

STEM

PACKING NUT

BONNET

BODY

GATE

Inside a gate valve.

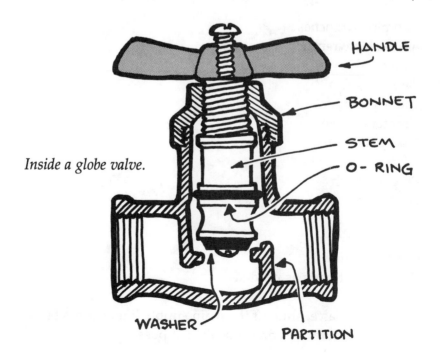

HANDLE

BONNET

STEM

O-RING

Inside a globe valve.

WASHER

PARTITION

When repairing shutoff valves, you might need to use a propane torch. If you do use a propane torch, please take the following precautions:

1. Remember that propane fuel is extremely flammable.
2. Always follow the operating instructions that come with the torch.
3 Use the torch only in a well-ventilated area.
4. Protect any flammable surrounding materials with a fireproof shield.
5. Disconnect the cylinder from the valve when the torch is not in use.
6. Do not store the propane tank near heat or in an inhabited room.

Tools & Materials

☐ Two pipe wrenches
☐ Adjustable wrench
☐ Wire brush
☐ Safety goggles
☐ Safety gloves
☐ Fireproof shield
☐ Emery cloth
☐ Pliers
☐ Propane torch
☐ Union
☐ Hacksaw
☐ Compression ring
☐ Coupling nut
☐ Replacement parts as needed

To repair a valve, shut off the main supply line, open a faucet to relieve any pressure, and drain the lines if possible.

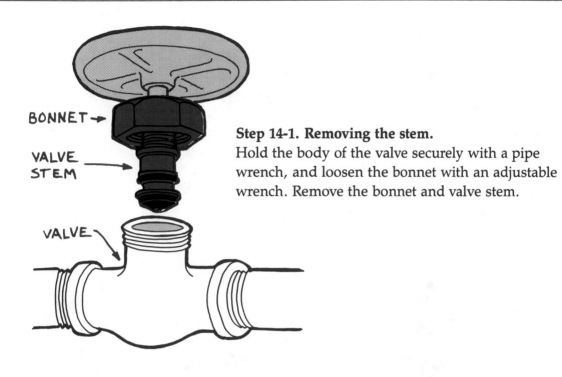

BONNET →

VALVE STEM →

VALVE

Step 14-1. Removing the stem.
Hold the body of the valve securely with a pipe wrench, and loosen the bonnet with an adjustable wrench. Remove the bonnet and valve stem.

Step 14-2. Repairing the valve.
Thoroughly scour the inside of the valve body with a wire brush. Now replace any washer, O-ring, or packing, and reassemble the valve. If the valve is still faulty, replace it.

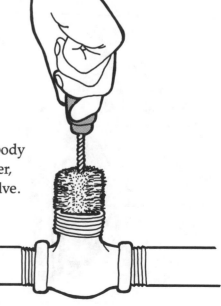

Step 14-3. Removing the valve.

Remove the bonnet and valve stem. If the valve is threaded, use two wrenches and remove the union. If the valve has no union, you'll have to cut the pipe on one side of the valve. Then unscrew the valve from the other pipe. (See chapter 13.) If the valve is soldered in place, wear safety goggles and gloves and use a fireproof shield to protect any flammable material. With pliers, hold the pipe while you heat the joint with a propane torch. When the solder starts to run, pull the pipe from the valve body. Now heat the other joint and remove the valve body from the pipe.

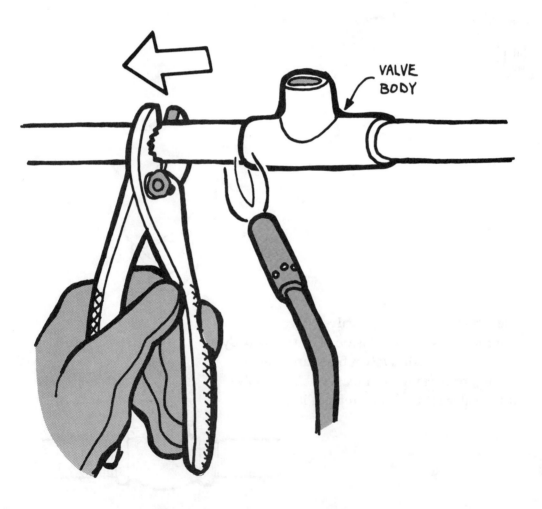

VALVE BODY

Step 14-4. Replacing a threaded valve.
On a threaded valve, apply pipe tape to the threads and screw the valve in place by hand. Hold the pipe with a pipe wrench, and tighten the valve with another wrench. Thread a new piece of pipe into the open end of the valve and install a union.

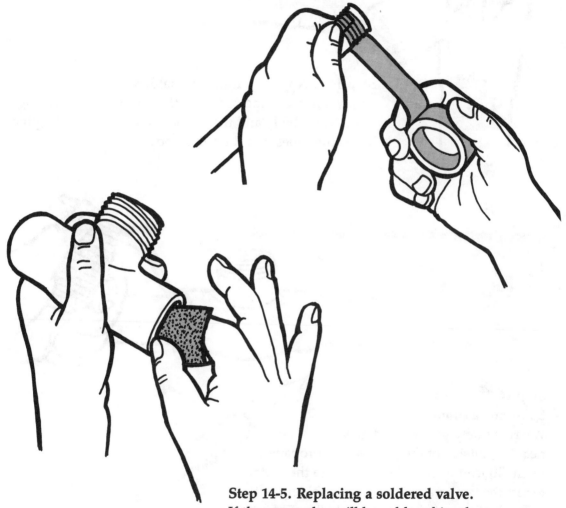

Step 14-5. Replacing a soldered valve.
If the new valve will be soldered in place, remove the bonnet and valve stem from the valve. Clean the ends of the pipe and the open ends of the valve body with emery cloth or a wire brush. The metal should shine brightly.

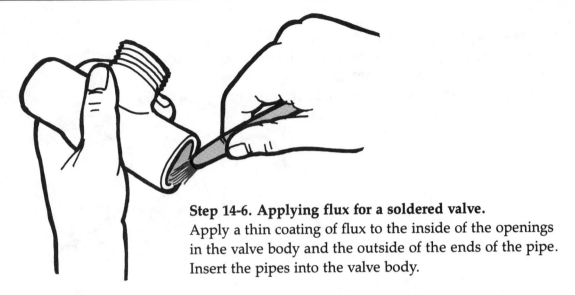

Step 14-6. Applying flux for a soldered valve.
Apply a thin coating of flux to the inside of the openings
in the valve body and the outside of the ends of the pipe.
Insert the pipes into the valve body.

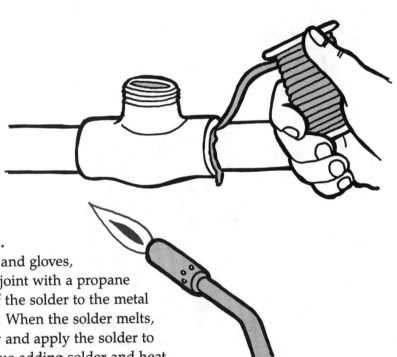

Step 14-7.
Soldering a connection.
Wearing safety goggles and gloves,
heat the outside of the joint with a propane
torch. Touch the end of the solder to the metal
to test the temperature. When the solder melts,
move the flame slightly and apply the solder to
the connection. Continue adding solder and heat
until the connection is completely filled with solder
and starts to drip. Repeat the soldering steps on the
other joint and wipe off any burnt flux with a wet rag.

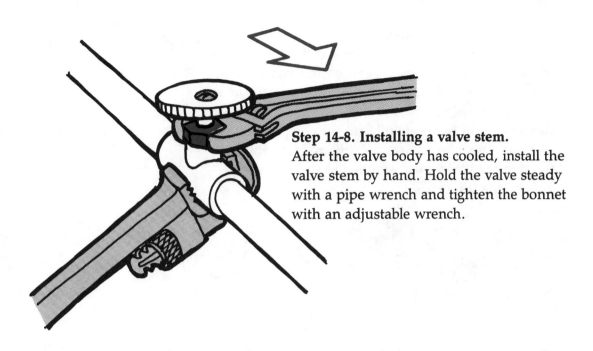

Step 14-8. Installing a valve stem.
After the valve body has cooled, install the valve stem by hand. Hold the valve steady with a pipe wrench and tighten the bonnet with an adjustable wrench.

Step 14-9.
Installing a fixture shutoff valve.
First, shut off the main water supply line and open a faucet to relieve the pressure.

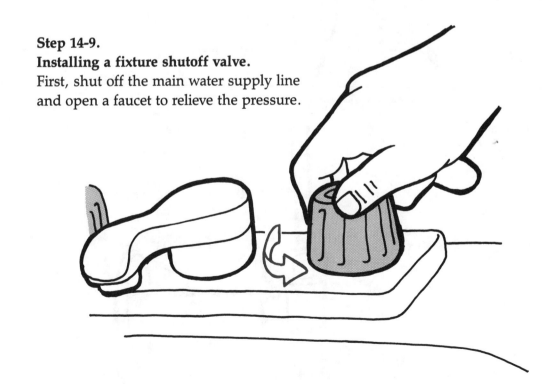

Step 14-10. Disconnecting the supply tube.
Use an adjustable wrench to disconnect the supply tube
from the *stub-out* in the wall. Use a basin wrench to
disconnect the supply tube from the bottom of the faucet.
Remove the fitting on the stub-out and slide the nut back
close to the wall. Now carefully cut the compression ring
with a hacksaw, and remove the ring from the stub-out.
If the stub-out is threaded, simply use two wrenches
to remove the fitting.

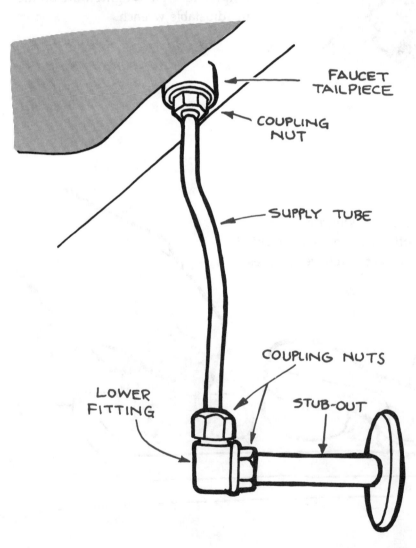

FAUCET
TAILPIECE

COUPLING
NUT

SUPPLY TUBE

COUPLING NUTS

LOWER
FITTING

STUB-OUT

Step 14-11. Installing the new valve.

Slide the coupling nut and compression ring of the new valve
onto the stub-out. Next, slide the opening in the valve onto the
end of the stub-out. Press it on the stub-out as far as it will go.
Align the outlet of the valve up toward the faucet.

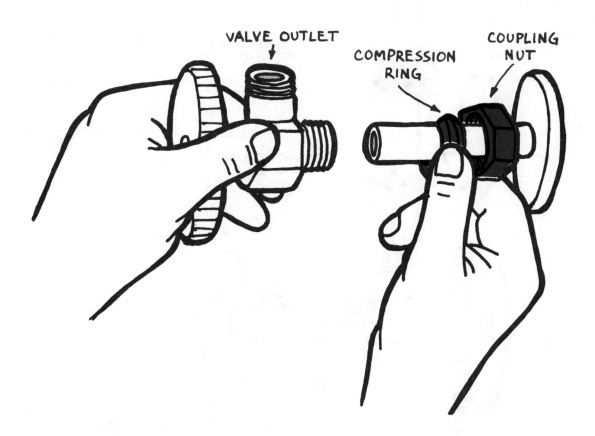

VALVE OUTLET   COMPRESSION RING   COUPLING NUT

Step 14-12. Completing the job.

Slide the compression ring from the stub-out against the valve opening and tighten the coupling nut by hand. Hold the valve steady with a wrench and tighten the coupling nut with another wrench. If the stub-out is threaded, wrap the threads with pipe tape and install the valve. If the valve is to be soldered, remove the stem, clean the joints, apply the solder, and, when the solder has cooled, reinstall the stem. Reconnect the old supply tube to the valve, or replace the tube with a new one. To reconnect the tube, slide the compression ring down the tube and tighten the coupling nut as before. Turn the water back on.

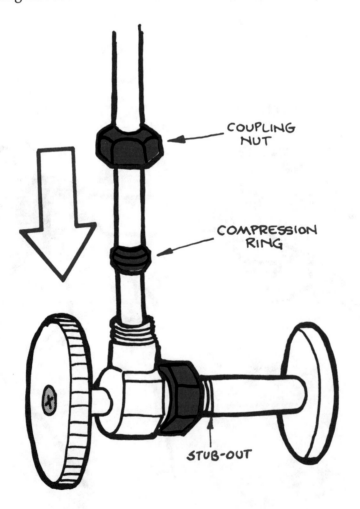

Glossary

aerator   A device attached to a faucet spout that introduces air into the flow of water to prevent the water from splashing.

ball cock   A valve that is operated by a lever and that has a floating ball.

ball faucet   A single-lever faucet that uses a hollow brass ball with holes to control the flow of water; also called a *single-lever faucet*.

ball flush valve   A ball-shaped stopper in a toilet used to release water from the tank to the bowl.

C-clamp   A C-shaped device, with a threaded shaft, that is used to grip something.

ceramic-disc cartridge   A type of single-lever faucet that has a cartridge containing two ceramic discs for controlling the flow of water.

clevis screw   A screw used to fasten the U-shaped end of a strap with holes in it.

clevis strap
A metal strap with holes that is used to fasten one thing to another.

coupling nut   A slip nut used to join two pieces of pipe.

diverter valve   A selector valve that can switch the flow of water from a faucet spout to a spray head.

CIRCUIT BREAKER

electrical panel
The electrical service entrance panel
that contains the circuit breakers.

emery cloth A cloth coated with powdered emery
(a variety of corundum) for cleaning metals.

faucet seat
The tapered faucet opening rim
that a washer presses against.

fixture Any attachment, such as a sink, shower, tub,
or toilet, considered to be part of the house.

flapper flush valve
A flapper valve is used in a toilet to release
water from the tank to the bowl.

gasket
A piece of material placed in
a joint to make it leakproof.

gate valve A valve that uses a movable disc
to control the flow of water. A gate valve
is used as a main shutoff valve.

globe valve
A valve with a spherical chamber
that uses a washer and a seat
to regulate the flow of water.

hex wrench
A wrench designed
for a six-sided fitting;
also called a seat wrench.

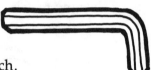

locknut
A nut connection used to hold a fitting
to a fixture or another fitting.

main valve   The main shutoff valve controlling the flow of water
to the house.

O-ring
A smooth, flexible ring,
sometimes rubber, used
in a groove to create a seal.

packing material   A self-forming material
used to create a seal around the stem of a faucet.

packing washer   A rubber washer used to create a seal around the stem of a faucet.

pivot rod
The rod connected to a stopper that opens and closes a drain.

setscrew
A screw used to prevent movement between one part and another.

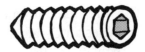

shutoff valve
A valve used to control the flow of water. Usually fully opened or closed.

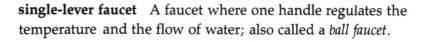

single-lever faucet   A faucet where one handle regulates the temperature and the flow of water; also called a *ball faucet*.

sleeve cartridge

A cartridge that has a movable sleeve with holes in it, used in one type of single-lever faucet to regulate the temperature and flow of water.

stem

The threaded part of a faucet that uses an O-ring and a washer to regulate the flow of water.

stem faucet

A faucet that uses a stem to regulate the flow of water.

stub-out

The stub end of a tube or pipe that extends from the wall.

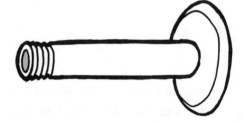

tailpiece
A section of pipe that connects to the bottom of a drain.

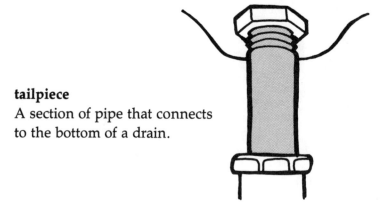

trap
A U-shaped piece of pipe in a drain, filled with water, used to prevent fumes from escaping.

vent stack
A section of pipe extending from the drain up through the roof to equalize air pressure.

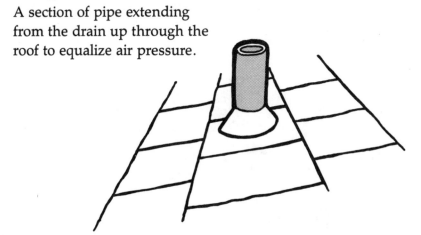

Index